The Management Option

The
Management
Option

Nine Strategies for Leadership

David L. Sudhalter, Ph.D.

Boston State College
Boston, Massachusetts

HUMAN SCIENCES PRESS
72 Fifth Avenue   3 Henrietta Street
NEW YORK, NY 10011 ● LONDON, WC2E 8LU

Copyright © 1980 by Human Sciences Press, Inc.
72 Fifth Avenue, New York, New York 10011

Printed in the United States of America
0123456789   987654321

Library of Congress Cataloging in Publication Data

Sudhalter, David L

   The management option.

   Includes index.
   1. Management. 2. Leadership. I. Title.
HD31.S75   658   LC 80-12992
ISBN 0-87705-084-8
ISBN 0-87705-089-9 (paper)

For Annette, Reba, and Sam

Contents

FOREWORD   9

INTRODUCTION   11

1. POWER   17
   The Uses—and Abuses—of Power
   Is Machiavelli for You?
   E Pluribus Unum
   Shaking Things Up a Bit
   The Lost Art of Communicating

2. LUCK   38
   The Challenge of Change
   Review the Past
   Make a Wish
   The Nature—and Power—of
   Positive Thinking

3. ABILITY   62
   Top Executives Don't Always Stay
   on Top
   Born to Rule?
   Beyond the Purple Haze
   Discover Your Ability

4. NONCONFORMITY   89
   Don't Be a Clone
   It's Their Style That Beguiles
   Even Fish Swim Upstream

5. TIMING   116
   The Pregnancy of Time
   Opportunity River
   Where Did the Time Go?
   A Man With a Plan

6. OBJECTIVES   141
   Be All That You Can Be
   The Biggest Job of All
   How the Object Becomes the
   Subject

7. WE   168
   Telling the Trees from the Forest
   Old Wine in New Bottles
   The Empires of the Future Are the
   Empires of the Mind

8. IMAGINATION   195
   The Eureka Complex
   How Do You Get There From Here?
   Road Blocks to Creativity
   The Creative Organization
   Once Upon a Time . . .
   What's Your I.Q.?

9. Now!   224
   It's Moving Time
   Show and Tell
   The Climb from Within
   Measure for Measure

INDEX   247

Foreword

$\mathcal{N}$owhere else in the world has management science reached such heightened development as it has in the United States. American management science has pioneered in the use of sophisticated techniques such as computer technology, the use of cybernetics, and the integration of managerial techniques with the mathematical sciences. Yet, despite all of these innovative developments, which have made the American schools of management models for the rest of the world, there have remained certain unsolved enigmas that continue to bedevil those who are on the way up the ladder as well as those who have already arrived at the top. These enigmas concern the roles that such ephemeral qualities as power, luck, nonconformity, and timing play in their lives. This book was conceived to provide at least a few of the answers to the age-old dilemmas that face every person who suddenly has leadership and its responsibilities thrust upon him or her. It also should make the aspiring leader of an organization more cognizant and more sensitive to the world around him or her. Admittedly, I have tried to discuss some very difficult topics, but from my own years of teaching and experience, I came to the conclusion that these topics have been ignored for too long. Moreover, many of them have been hitherto presented in only a piecemeal fashion.

As a result, this book was conceived for both the practitioner and the novice in the field of managerial science. The subjects that I have chosen apply equally to all kinds of management and organizations, private as well as public, for the greatest need that mankind has today is the need for excellent and thoughtful managers. We have witnessed colossal blunders and errors that are magnified a thousand times more than a few decades ago, because we are playing for much higher stakes. We are tinkering more with our environment, our future development, and our economy than any other generation in history. All of this new experimentation will require leadership that is thoughtful, sensitive, and most of all, future-oriented.

A number of people have inspired and helped me in the preparation of this book. My wife, Annette, who considerately saw to it that I had the time to complete the manuscript, and who read it critically, deserves much of the credit for its successful completion. My colleagues, A. Collins Jenko, Winston Langley, Robert Weiner, and George Berkley were extremely generous with their time. Their comments and criticism proved to be most valuable to me, and without their objectivity, the book would not have reached fruition. I am also indebted to the person who gave me a great deal of encouragement, guidance, and help early in my career, Professor Andrew Gyorgy. Mr. Robert L. Bernstein, President of Hope Chemical Corporation and a past Governor of the Kiwanis, was kind enough to read part of the manuscript, and his comments from the point of view of a business executive proved to be most helpful. Finally, I must also thank the administration and staff of Boston State College for creating the kind of friendly and supportive atmosphere that makes it all possible.

David L. Sudhalter
Needham, Massachusetts
October 10, 1979

Introduction

Do you want to be a leader? Or a follower? If you have read this far, you want to become a leader. The question is, how? No one is a "born" leader. People who become executives have learned the art of leading and inspiring others. Those are the people who are not content to belong to the mob of followers, but rather want to become part of that most precious and rarest of commodities that the world hungers for so much today—executive leadership. You, too, will reap the rich rewards of successful leadership by learning and acquiring the techniques outlined in this book. Until recently, people believed that to achieve executive status, one had to do so by manipulating others, or one had to be tricky or cunning. But new evidence has shown that by applying the recently discovered principles of leadership and management, you can not only *reach* the top, but acquire the means to *stay* there.

Napoleon's famous remark, "Every soldier in my army carries a Marshal's Baton in his knapsack . . ."* was never truer than it is today. You, too, have the potential of leadership and executive ability within you. What is needed now is to bring these qualities out into the open and make them work for you. This chemistry will be explained in the following chapters as a formula that anyone can follow. The formula for success in leadership is: *Plan to win.* That is, *your* plan to win: *Power, luck, ability, nonconformity, timing, objectives, we not me, imagination, now!* This formula will become your battle plan for success in achieving executive leadership. By absorbing the lessons

---

**The Macmillan Book of Proverbs, Maxims, and Famous Phrases.* The Macmillan Company, New York, 1948.

associated with this formula, your *plan to win* will begin to emerge and grow as you develop into the kind of leader who can direct people and command the respect and admiration of others. That will be one result of your newly acquired abilities of leadership. You will also acquire the ten qualities that all good leaders have:

1. To be able to inspire and motivate others.
2. To be able to delegate authority at the right times, to the right people, and under the right conditions.
3. To be able to see at least just around the next corner, by developing your powers of perception.
4. To be able to plan and organize the activities of your organization. Such ability to plan usually begins with yourself.
5. To have the ability to maintain harmony and equilibrium in an organization.
6. To be able to assume the responsibility for the organization, not only when things go well, but when they go badly, and still come off looking like a hero.
7. To be a spokesman for your subordinates as well as for your organization.
8. To be able to negotiate effectively.
9. To be able to manage a crisis calmly.
10. To be able to set goals that are realistic and attainable.

Most people would like to set their sights on becoming executives, but they are afraid to. Many of the reasons that they give sound familiar, but are simply not valid for denying oneself a richly rewarding career as a leader of others. Do any of these excuses sound familiar?:

"It's a matter of luck—and I'm not lucky."
"I don't have the drive."
"I would have to give up too much of my time and personal life."
"I don't have the guts for it."
"I'm too easygoing to be an executive."

These are all *excuses,* not *reasons* for denying yourself access to the exciting world of executive leadership.

There is a common misconception that to become a leader, one must change his personality. Nonsense! You are a unique human being with special and highly prized attributes. The problem really is how to get those special qualities of yours working *for* you, not against you. That does not require a change of personality, but the resourceful channeling of the special and marvelous qualities that you already possess. What we must do, therefore, is to learn to direct and channel our energies so that skillful leadership will become second nature. Remember, leadership is a skill that can be learned, and its secrets will yield only to those who want to become leaders.

The formula, *plan to win,* should be thought of as a set of guideposts on the highway of successful leadership. These guideposts will not only get you to your goal; they will sustain you along the way, and make it easy for you to retrace your steps any time that you may need a reappraisal of your activities. Each of these guideposts has significance for the role of the leader. *Power* can be used either successfully or abused with disastrous results, for power means responsibility, as well as control over others. *Luck* is not, as most people believe, something that shows up only in your horoscope. Remember the fable of Aladdin's Lamp? The lamp lay there, a useless piece of junk for centuries, until Aladdin came along. This fable really tells us that we can enhance our opportunities and twist fortune's arm, if we will but try. *Ability* to lead is not the same as ability to manage. The latter means technical expertise. The ability to lead is something altogether different. It is a portable and universal skill that can be applied in almost any environment with great success once you have mastered the skills of leading. *Nonconformity* is the mark of the leader, the self-starter, the doer, the innovator. Without the nonconformist rocking the boat, there would be no new starts, no new ideas, and worst of all, no progress. *Timing* is another one of those qualities long considered to be ephemeral. But that is also a myth.

Good timing is part of a successful leader's baggage. In fact, it is an indispensable tool of his trade, and as will be seen, timing can both be learned and improved upon. *Objectives* and the ability to define them, as well as to make them part of a rational plan of action are essential for the leader. Without the ability to establish a priority of objectives and goals, we cannot develop a rational plan of leadership and management. *We, not me* signifies that one of the chief requirements of leadership is an understanding of how organizations function. Getting people to think in terms of organizational survival is one of the greatest challenges that you will ever face. *Imagination* means that we must use our ideas and our imaginations in a constructive way. Moreover, as leaders, we must learn how to develop the imaginations of those around us. The creative forces within the organization that we lead must all be put to effective use. *Now* is the time. Time that you put your plan to win into action. The world is full of dreamers and procrastinators. As a leader of others, you will stand out as one who causes activity to happen.

These, then, are the ingredients for success in leadership. Put together properly and well coordinated, they will open up exciting new vistas for you. Opportunities that you never dreamed of will suddenly become attainable as your eyes are opened and you begin to understand the meaning of successful leadership. Such leadership cannot be yours, however, without effort. You must do your part as well, and the following chapters must be seen as both instruction and exercise. Absorb the instruction, but practice the exercises as well.

Finally, there are real benefits to be gained from becoming a successful leader. A few are listed below:

Health. Most studies have shown that executives and their families enjoy better health, look better, live longer, and have better mental health than the rest of the population. They also lead more varied and interesting lives. The old myths about executives having ulcers and heart attacks are just that—old myths. The fact is that executives are more careful about their health, and are more aware of the risks and dangers of stress than any other segment of the population. Most American corporations spend large amounts of money for checkups and medical care for their executives. Many have even gone one step further and have installed exercise rooms and tennis and squash courts so that their executives can have recreation at their place of work. The real truth is that it is the lower echelon workers who suffer more from stress and heart disease.

Money. Your earnings will rise as you move up the ladder of responsibility. So will your fringe benefits. Moreover, you will be able to change jobs more easily than before. Even the executive recruiters, better known as "headhunters" will be coming after you. Have you ever taken note of the growing number of these agencies? They are engaged in a constant search for executive talent. Why? Because the chronic shortage of executive leaders is the greatest hunger that afflicts America—and the world. Indeed, high paying executive jobs are going begging every day of the week. Even the federal government has adopted a new merit system whereby it will search for executive talent, and will give bonuses to executives who have proven their ability to lead. So even the leaders of the United States have come to the realization that patronage and nepotism are not substitutes for executive excellence.

Confidence. As you rise to a position of leadership, you will acquire more self-confidence than you ever dreamed you could have. You will see a new person emerging, and by the way, you will find that many of the fears that you may now have will evaporate as self-confidence increases. Self-confidence increases self-respect and will quickly earn the respect of those around you.

Change. Leadership gives us the opportunity to effect change. Have you ever thought that you could do a much better job than your boss? I have, often. And when I got the chance, I discovered that I *could* do a much better job. A friend of mine, who has held a number of responsible positions with public agencies, had lunch with me recently. I asked him what motivated him to continually seek positions of leadership. He replied, "I have the chance to put my ideas into effect—and I think that I can do a better job than the previous management." Change is exciting, and the opportunity to become an agent of change will be yours if you choose the path of leadership. The feeling of creativity that results from being able to effect change is one of the greatest rewards a human being can have. Indeed, the executive who has made successful innovations or changes must feel like the football quarterback, making a touchdown after a 45-yard run. Executives who are in there making changes are exciting people who lead interesting lives; they are the lucky ones.

By now, you are eager to set about becoming Number One! So, let's get on with it!

1

Power

The Uses—and Abuses—of Power

Apart from the destructive power of nature, the power that one human being can have over others is the most awesome fact of life. Since the beginning of time, men have feared, admired, and respected power. Consider the following kinds of power, and then ask yourself if there is any force that is greater in human affairs today:

Positive Aspects	*Negative Aspects*
Power creates	Power destroys
Power builds	Power corrupts
Power inspires	Power intimidates
Power renews	Power terrorizes
Power rewards	Power punishes

Those who have power over others can use their power for constructive—or destructive—ends. Power must be used carefully, for it is potential dynamite in the hands of a capricious or arbitrary person. Everyone who wants or has power must consider several ground rules or basic facts about power.

First, no power is limitless. While it may seem to us that the executive or the boss has this kind of power, some careful reflection will lead us to the realization that those in positions of authority always have someone above them to answer to. In corporations, the executives have to answer to their boards of directors and to their shareholders. In institutions, the leaders have their boards of trustees, etc. to answer to. In government, politicians have to answer to their constituents, and these days, it seems everyone has to answer to a government bureaucrat. So we all exist in a great chain of command, and even though we mistakenly see those in authority above us as some kind of omnipotent god in human form, we have to realize that it just isn't so. Our omnipotent leaders, it turns out, have feet of clay just like us, and they have to answer to someone else just as we do.

Second, power over others is a temporary state. It is delegated or loaned only for the term of *successful* leadership, and will be withdrawn when the leader fails to make proper use of it. Unfortunately, we often come to think of someone's hold on power as a permanent phenomenon. Nothing could be further from the truth. One of the first things that you must do, therefore, is forget the idea that power is some kind of a lifetime sinecure. It may seem so at times, but history has shown that great empires, financial and political, have fallen into oblivion, and with them, their once all-powerful leaders and executives. Think, then, of power as something that is loaned to the user, but is subject to withdrawal for any number of reasons. Those who hold power are really the keepers of a trust, and will hold it only as long as they are trusted. This is a fact of life that is becoming increasingly important in the corporate and organizational world of today.

Third, the power to lead is closely related to the environment in which that power flourishes. Think of power as a form of energy that derives its strength and drive from its environment. It is thus the people around the leader who give him of their energy. Their support energizes the leader, keeps up his drive and enthusiasm, and galvanizes him into action. Without the support of those below him, the leader is like a rudderless ship. So all heads of organizations exist in a kind of symbiotic relationship with those around them. Power is a driving and moving force whose energy comes from the organization that it controls and directs.

Fourth, power is only *potential* power until it is used, and even then, its usefulness depends on the skill and initiative of the wielder of power. He shapes and molds it, and makes it work for the organization. But remember that the power to lead is potential power only; it is only what we make of that potential that defines the amount of power that we may have. Sometimes, such potential develops in strange ways. A young friend of mine who was an executive with a major U.S. corporation was asked to form a new division; he was given a budget and complete control over his new division with the proviso that he must have a successful division within five years. My friend was successful, and now the tail wags the dog. The new division has proven to be a major source of capital for the older parent company, and the management of the new division has become a controlling and directing force for the old master.

In the case mentioned above, the power to lead and organize a new division was dormant until my friend came along and put it to work. There used to be a saying among the new immigrants to America that the streets were paved with gold. All one had to do to become a millionaire was to stoop down and fill his pockets. What they should have said instead was that in America the streets are paved with power—it's there waiting for you. The opportunity to lead must be recognized in its embryonic state, while the ability to use that opportunity requires the imagination and decisiveness that is normally associated with the successful use of power. Power is wielded successfully only by those who decide to *use* it. Remember, we are all potential users of power from the day we are born.

Fifth, with power comes obligation. It obliges the holder of power to relate to those beneath and above him. It obligates him to communicate and to consult. Think of the total power of an organization as a huge wheel. The rim of the wheel represents the workers; the spokes, the executives; and the hub, the top echelon. No part of this wheel could exist or function without the other parts. They are all held together by the tensions and forces that we call power. How well they are held together depends on the ability of the parts of our wheel to relate to each other in an orderly and integrated fashion. In any organization, then, the parts must relate to the whole. That is why the idea of power as an obligation is important. This is what makes power responsible and impresses the leader with the need to relate to those next to him in the hierarchy of the organization. Obligation thus means responsibility. All leaders must bear the responsibility for their actions, and only by seeing themselves as part of the total structure of power of their organization can they properly place their own areas of obligation.

Finally, power can be centralized or dispersed. Centralized power means that the leadership alone makes the decisions. The leadership can be concentrated in one person or in a few persons. The point is, however, that decision making takes place only at the top when power is centralized. Conversely, when power is diffused or dispersed, decision making becomes a sharing process. The sharing also means that the responsibility for decisions must be shared. Which is better? The late Howard Hughes was the best example of highly centralized decision making in a large financial empire. Henry Ford I was another example. In both cases, near disaster almost overtook the organizations that they were running because neither man would share his decisions with associates. Today, most corporate management is based on shared decision-making power, because shared responsibility tends to increase the interest and enthusiasm of the people who can best make the organization a success—lower and middle level management. The leader of the organization is a catalyst. He prompts action in others; he inspires; he enthuses. The leader cannot fulfill these roles completely, however, unless there is some sharing of power. And if there is no diffusion of power, the energy of associates on the lower levels will not become available. Whereas most would agree in principle with the above statements on the need to share power, few really want to practice the idea with any degree of consistency. On assuming the leadership of an organization, everyone starts out with the best intentions of wanting to be "democratic," but soon lose their enthusiasm for democracy; and that is why power has the very peculiar habit of always wanting to move toward greater centralization. In order to maintain some kind of balance in this process, therefore, one must always try to guard against those tendencies. The more absolute and centralized power becomes, the less rational and intelligent will be the decision-making process, and the chance that the organization will fail becomes that much greater.

Power is a difficult concept to comprehend. But, as we have seen, it is an awesome and mighty force that can build empires or destroy them just as quickly if not wisely used. There are many roads to the acquisition of power. Let us next consider a few of them.

Is Machiavelli for You?

Niccolo Machiavelli (1469–1527) was a Florentine philosopher and writer whose name has become a synonym for achieving power through any means. The adjective "Machiavellian" has become a household word that stands for perfidy, treachery, and the manipulation of others to gain one's ends. Machiavelli was a victim of his times; he lost his political job and was driven into exile at the age of 43; and then as today, who wants a 43-year-old has-been, when there are younger men around? At any rate, Machiavelli wanted to make a comeback, and become a political adviser to the powerful Medici family.

He wrote two treatises (*The Prince* and *The Discourses*) and hoped that his unsolicited advice would endear him to the new rulers of Florence. Machiavelli urged the use of unscrupulous and cruel methods by means of which a person could rise to power and hold it. These were bad times for Italy, and principalities were being turned over more quickly than a chain of fast food restaurants. Machiavelli's advice was to urge the neophyte prince to use any and all methods that would help him to gain and retain his power, especially if he was new to the neighborhood. For example, he advised that,

> a prince, and especially a new prince, cannot observe all those things which are considered good in men, being often obliged, in order to maintain the state, to act against faith, against charity, against humanity, and against religion.[1]

Machiavelli never did get back into the good graces of the Medici family. Instead, he was ridiculed by his friends and contemporaries and forced to eke out an existence as a broken-down playwright in the final years of his life. Machiavelli may have been derided and ridiculed in his lifetime, but in some ways he may have had the last laugh, for he saw how men wielded power, and simply was telling it as he saw it. He tried to justify the use of these immoral methods on the grounds that they would be used for noble ends—the preservation of the harmony of the state (translated today into the preservation of the corporation or the public agency, etc.). Was Machiavelli right? Should we gain power by using fraud, deceit, trickery, or other immoral means? Does the end justify any means? While such tactics may bring us to the brink of power, they will not see us over the top. Moreover, the Machiavellian methods that we may use in achieving the top job may turn out to be an albatross around our necks instead of an asset to our careers. There is another danger inherent in the use of Machiavellian tactics. Once they are used as a means for gaining the leadership, they tend to become institutionalized. That is, they become part of the *modus operandi* of the organization, and everyone wants to mimic the successful practitioner of high tricks and low tactics. These practices become self-destructive, as they are turned against the person who decided to use them in the first place, and they are bound to backfire. So, while Machiavelli's ideas present an "easy" road to quick success, his enthusiastic followers will soon find themselves following a road that is paved with thorns.

In recent years, there has been quite a revival in Machiavellianism, but with a more sophisticated psychological twist to it. This school of thought is busy advising people as to how they can learn to manipulate others, and by becoming amateur psychologists, how they can "psych out" other people and read their thoughts. Much of this belongs in what one might refer to as the "subliminal" school of behavior, because this kind of person employs tactics that deal with the subconscious rather than taking conscious behavior at face value. Appealing to the subconscious drives and needs of others, including the boss, can also produce disastrous results and monstrous miscalculations because we are amateurs at it, not trained psychologists or psychiatrists. Manipulating others' needs and drives is a dangerous and risky game. Yet, in recent years, there has been a plethora of books and articles that advise us to do just that. One author will tell you that you must stand in a certain way at a cocktail party, so as to make the right impression. We are taught how to read others' minds by the way they fold their arms or cross their legs; young women are taught how to put on the appropriate "come hither" look to achieve success, and so on. While these parlor games are great fun, they are not for the serious person who wants to rise to the leadership of his organization. We cannot manipulate the behavior of others; the best we can do is try to modify our own behavior in areas that we feel will be helpful. Machiavellian tactics are great for the Machiavellian, but people who want to be accepted for what they are should not use such tactics. However, all is not lost, and our old friend Machiavelli may have done us a good turn after all, because we can use his methods to identify the typologies of certain kinds of people who may be harmful to our careers and futures. We cannot do much about the fact that we are thrown in to work with a group of people not of our choosing, but we can do a great deal about whom we choose to associate with, and what kinds of people to look out for, because what we say and whom we associate with from the office will probably have a great deal of influence on our chances for advancement to the leadership. We are in a sense married to the organization and to our fellow workers, and we really cannot escape them by remaining aloof. Therefore, we must exercise discretion and caution, and know our fellow workers for what they are. Herewith is a typology of some of the common personalities and traits that can be found among the people who work for every organization, including management people as well as the rank and file:

Agent 007.   This person is otherwise known as the company spy. This person suffers from great insecurity and he or she feels that the only way to stay in the boss' good favor is to try to be his eyes and ears. Unfortunately, some executives encourage this practice; and that is why it is so prevalent. Agent 007 is thus preying on the boss' weakness for secret information. Every organization has an Agent 007; find out who he or she is in yours, be careful what you say in front of him or her, and *never* share any confidences with that person. It will be back to the boss in a matter of minutes. Luckily, there only seems to be one spy per office as a rule. The competition must be keen! So your task is made relatively simple. Just find the right one.

The Grand Inquisitor.   Every organization has one of these also. The Grand Inquisitor will pump you dry of information, but will give you none in return. He or she will try to get out of you all that you know, and everything about yourself. They soon become walking file cabinets loaded with information on everyone who is foolish enough to make revelations to them. Learn how to turn aside a question by asking a question, and you will soon find out that the Grand Inquisitor will drop you and quickly go on to another victim.

The Sycophant. This person is so busy flattering others and appealing to their sense of vanity that he has no time to worry about his own future, and it is grim indeed, for people just don't take warmly to servile or obsequious individuals. Flattery and the affirmation of others is fine when they are deserved, but don't let your head get turned, especially if you are in a position of responsibility or authority, or the sycophant will get you if you don't watch out.

The Comedian. Again, a standard in every office. A great person, hail and well met. Loads of fun, but stay away from him or you'll soon enjoy the same label yourself. And you know what happens to comedians—they run out of jokes and they're soon out of the running.

Doomsday Dan. This is a sincere person who is just a born pessimist. He believes along with Murphy that if anything can possibly go wrong, it will. He is a purveyor of gloom and doom, and a great one to have around on a dismal day. Again, Doomsday Dans are standard equipment for every organization. Learn to stay away from this type of person, as he will finally make a convert of you and ruin whatever optimism you may have come into the world with.

The Critic. Like Doomsday Dan, the critic finds much that is wrong and little that is right. Criticism has its place in the world, but this person is a walking supermarket of criticism! He will criticize the boss, the customers, the board of directors, the employees, etc., until tears come to your eyes. Not only that, but Agent 007 will overhear him, and if you happen to be a confidant, you may become guilty by association. So stay away from The Critic, and don't even try to convert him—he'll never change.

By now, you're probably saying to yourself, who's left? Everyone in my office has been described. Not so. There are plenty of healthy personalities left in your office. Search them out and befriend them. But never fall in with the kinds of people who will set your career back. Also, learn to be a listener, not a talker. Remember, we are master of the words yet unspoken, but the words that are spoken will soon become our master.

Our friend Machiavelli, it turns out, was halfway right. It pays to know the seamy tactics that others use so that we will not fall into the trap of using them ourselves. Within your organization, you will be known for the company that you keep. In fact, those above you are watching, and it is all the more important for your climb to the leadership that you cultivate relationships within the organization that will improve your image. The power to choose your relationships is a power that must not be overlooked by you, for choosing the wrong associates can seriously weaken your bid for a position of leadership. Indeed, it can be pointed out that you are a mirror image of those with whom you associate. Exercising control, therefore, over your associations must be seen as your first act of power, because it is a conscious act of your will.

The first key to the acquisition of power, then, is in choosing the right associates. They will enhance your reputation, and your progress toward your goal will be that much faster. The alliances that you may be forming now will become very important to your future progress. Let us now consider the next step in the climb to power.

E PLURIBUS UNUM

The national motto of the United States is *e pluribus unum,* which means "from many into one." It is a fitting motto for businesses as well, for it implies teamwork—the teamwork that is essential for the harmony of an organization. Your role as a member of the team is much more important at this stage of your life than trying to express yourself as an individual. Through teamwork, you will be noticed much faster, if you apply yourself accordingly. But first, we must understand what is meant by the concept of teamwork.

In a world where specialization has become increasingly important, modern management relies heavily on the practice of delegating authority and responsibility. The leadership turns over a percentage of its decision-making authority to a team. This team can be defined as either a department that has permanent status (long-range) or temporary status (short-range), which is assembled to solve a specific problem, after which it may go out of existence. Management practices vary a great deal as to how they assign or delegate their decision-making authority. Consider the variety of options that are available.

The first option is complete centralization of power and authority in the hands of the head of the department. Here there is less opportunity for collaboration and sharing with the rest of the department. Instead, the members of the group are made to feel more like automatons than thinking human beings. Such an approach is dehumanizing and bad for group morale. It also tends to be destructive because it stifles any initiative and prevents any good, constructive ideas from ever emerging from the group. The success of the group thus depends really on the ability of one person—the leader—to make the correct analysis and decisions. As we have seen before, the more centralized decision making is, the less rational it is, because we are all victims of our emotions and they frequently tend to blur our vision. The input from others becomes important to the ongoing rationality of any enterprise. A leader who does not solicit advice and opinions from subordinates is not a leader, for he is leading no one but himself.

The second type of team leadership is partially consultative. The boss still calls the shots and makes the decisions, but is explaining decisions to the members of the team. Such partial consultation is not much of an improvement over the first type because there is still no real input from the members of the team.

The third type of leadership is fully consultative. The boss or leader asks for and will receive suggestions and input from the members of the team. The leader can and does still reserve the right to make the final decisions, but agrees that he will explain those decisions as well as first listen carefully to any and all suggestions from the members of the team. Up to this point, our team still has a leader who has the authority and the final say in the decision-making process.

The fourth type of leadership is decentralized leadership. Here, decision making is shifted from the leader to the group, and with it, the responsibility for their actions and results. Such decentralization is inherently leaderless. The leader is merely the spokesman for the team, perhaps a first among equals, but no more than that. Moreover, with no way to fix or assign the responsibility to one person, *all* of the members of the team or group become equally guilty or responsible for any failures. Thus, an entire division or department could suffer when the blame for failure has to be shared. It takes a lot of initiative and collective wisdom for decentralized leadership to be effective. That is why it is not a very popular method of management, except for think tanks or other highly specialized activities where all members have equal input into decision making.

What mode is best for you? How will your ability to lead best be noticed? If there is any choice at all, the third mode (fully consultative) is probably the best environment in which to show off your potential as a leader. Here you can best have the opportunity to make the contributions that will bring you notice from the upper echelon. Here also, you will have more freedom to exercise your initiative. Thus, by choosing an environment in which you can express your ideas, you will probably achieve the greatest benefit to yourself.

There is yet another facet to the problem of teamwork, and that is the *size* of the team or group. Size affects the quality of work that a team will turn out; size will also affect the kind of leadership that the team has. The larger the group (over 20), the better are the chances that it can be guided and led because larger groups tend to need direction and leadership more than small ones. Conversely, the smaller the group (under 10), the greater are the chances that it will become unruly. This is because in small groups, factionalism and personality differences become more pronounced, whereas in large groups, such differences are quickly absorbed and tend to be submerged by the need for leadership. It is generally conceded that people do not work particularly well as a team when they are in small groups unless they are carefully chosen as to compatibility. Management, therefore, has to weigh personality factors carefully when it is assigning small groups of people to work together. The need to exercise such caution is more important than with larger teams.

Which size group is best for you? Smaller groups mean greater responsibility and more notice for you, but they also pose a greater challenge to your ability to get along with people and to resolve personality differences within the small team by acting as a middleman or peacemaker whenever factionalism or strife break out. Given a choice, the smaller team would probably present you with the greatest opportunity as well as the greatest challenge; after all, that's one of the chief reasons that we choose the path of leadership.

The second key in the climb to successful leadership is: *Choose the mode of organization that can best give you the opportunity to have your abilities noticed.*

Shaking Things up a Bit

Organizations, like people, go through crises. How well they weather a crisis has a lot to do with the ways in which power is used for what is usually called "crisis management." Most people avoid a crisis as though it were a plague, and you will see the weaker souls in your organization run quickly in the other direction when they see or smell a crisis situation approaching. But for someone like you, aiming for leadership, crisis is a golden opportunity to prove your worth, to step into the breach and become the hero of the hour. Remember the lines from Rudyard Kipling's poem, "If"?[2]

> If you can keep your head when all about you
> Are losing theirs and blaming it on you,
> If you can trust yourself when all men doubt you,
> But make allowance for their doubting too;
> If you can wait and not be tired by waiting,
> Yours is the Earth and everything that's in it,
> And—which is more—you'll be a Man, my son!

Crisis management will give you just the right opportunity to show your mettle and what is more, to break the normal routine of annual promotions, wait-your-turn-till-next-year put-downs, etc. So welcome the opportunity; it may be heaven-sent.

Crisis management not only gives us the opportunity to resolve problems; it also gives us the chance to be creative, improve, and reorient conditions more to our advantage. Remember, however, that all crises are temporary. We may often think that a particular crisis will never come to an end, but in reality crises are short-lived episodes in the life of any organization—episodes that can benefit you!

What kinds of crises might confront an organization? Whereas it is true that crises come in all shapes and sizes and usually strike when least expected, every organization is subjected to the strains and stresses of a crisis at least once a year. The problem lies in being able to identify the kind of crisis and in being able to deal with it calmly and rationally. There are really four identifiable kinds of crises that afflict most organizations:

Personnel. Of all the various crises that can afflict your organization, personnel problems are among the most common. Shortages of trained help, rapid shifts in needs, and unforeseen problems all take their toll. Added to this are the various labor-management tensions that can complicate the personnel picture. How could you benefit from a personnel crisis? Simple. Analyze your personnel situation and have answers ready for the boss when the crisis arrives. Everyone else will be running around wringing their hands. Not you! You will have some preparation and study under your belt. A young executive I know did just that. He studied the personnel records in his division and got to know how people with different skills could be shifted around to different tasks for temporary assignments until the crisis had passed. The young executive's calculations had proven correct, and his fellow junior executives were caught with their shirtsleeves down! Our young executive was the only one prepared to meet a crisis head-on and was able to take full advantage of this opportunity.

Leadership.   A leadership crisis can be among the most distressing of any of the calamities that can befall an organization. What should be your role as a rising hopeful leader? A change in the leadership usually produces a change in staff as well. It is possible to thus exploit a change in leadership to your advantage. This means again that you should prepare the groundwork for just such an eventuality. When you see a crisis in the leadership slowly building, you should have enough foresight to begin to prepare yourself to serve as one of the new assistants to the new leadership, which will be replacing the old, worn-out crew before long. So, the message again is watch for your opportunity, but prepare, *prepare, prepare!*

Environment.   A crisis in the environment can mean any crisis that is external to the organization, and something that takes place outside of its control. This kind of crisis can cause internal problems, of course, and here again is where golden opportunities lie in store for rising leaders. Learn to recognize the ramifications of these environmental crises, how they will affect your organization, and what steps could be taken to soften the impact. Study and analyze those external factors in your organization's environment, so that at the proper time you can be a walking encyclopedia of information. Just because your present job may not bring you outside of your organizational environment, that is not a reason for ignorance of the external world in which your organization has to survive. So become an expert on those problems and factors that are bound to have a far-reaching and serious effect on your organization's future (and yours).

Functional. A functional crisis is one in which the organization breaks down. For any number of reasons the usual method of organization has failed, and the firm or agency now needs to be reorganized. As in the other crisis situations, you can profit through preparation. Be aware of your organization's strengths and weaknesses by analyzing them. It has been well demonstrated in the past that at the time of reorganization or shakeups, as they are more commonly known, drastic changes can take place, and the top echelon frequently turns to middle level and lower level management for the answers. This becomes your chance to provide some interesting ideas and suggestions, *if you are prepared.*

Crisis management means that instead of going to pieces in an earthquake, the organization rolls with the tremors, whatever the cause, and lives to fight another day. This can only be accomplished if there is cool and rational judgment at the helm. Show the management that you are one of those kinds of people by preparing in advance for the days of crisis which always come.

The third key in the climb to successful management is: *Prepare, analyze, and study the various means by which any one of several crisis situations could be handled by your organization and be able to apply them if asked.*

The Lost Art of Communicating

Recently, a federal executive said to me, "I don't care about anything else—but send me people who can communicate!" Today corporations are hiring outside specialists and consultants to write their in-house communications because there are no people capable of doing the job within the organization. So the ability to communicate has assumed greater importance than ever before. Power cannot be effectively exercised unless there is adequate communication, for that is what makes up the central nervous core of any organization.

Consider what a communications breakdown would mean in your firm. Failure to communicate would make things pretty difficult indeed. But what you don't realize is that the present system now in use in your organization is probably quite inadequate to the needs. Here again, there are golden opportunities waiting for you. According to recent estimates, more than 80% of all firms are woefully inadequate in getting information to their employees in clear, understandable English. You could thus become indispensable by improving your communications skills. This might mean brushing up on everyday English usage, and learning to write clear, understandable memos instead of gobbledygook. You could also, starting from zero, attempt to reconstruct the communications network of your organization. There is probably a strong chance that you will find many gaps that could be filled, and your newly found expertise will undoubtedly endear you to the hearts of the leadership. Take a course in effective writing; build up your communications skills. They will turn out to be very valuable assets in today's market because many organizations have become so highly technical and overspecialized to the point that most of the primary skills have fallen by the wayside. That's why they have to go out and hire the kind of talent that *you* could be providing.

Communications is also the exercise of power. It is the method by which we make our wishes known and transmitted to others. Earlier, when I defined power, I purposely left out one very important definition. This definition of power has much to do with communication. Consider the fact that power can be defined as *controlled aggression.* Uncontrolled power is a destructive force, but power that is controlled and finely tuned by its holder can be used, conversely, for very creative purposes. In order for this to happen, power has to be communicated positively, not as an extension of brute force or as a series of

threats. Over the past few years, in fact, leading management specialists have all come to agree that the *last*
method to be used on the donkey is to beat him with a stick.
Ideas and motivation must come across with the least
amount of tension and hostility possible. That is when
controlled aggression becomes important. Only the mas-
terful leader can turn this kind of power that is so poten-
tially destructive into a creative and positive force. How?
By empathizing with those who are next on the ladder of
responsibility and by tapping the wellsprings of his own
humanity. Such empathy, when exhibited, will blunt the
most hostile and aggressive of adversaries. A kind word, a
kind gesture, therefore, will do more to communicate de-
sires and ideas than all the cursing, shouting, and plead-
ing in the world.

Nevertheless, we must admit that aggressiveness is a
necessary quality of executive life. Without it, there would
be little initiative, no competitiveness, and no progress.
But with aggressiveness come the green-eyed dragons of
jealousy and hostility and out goes all humanitarian attitudes. Those green-eyed dragons are not going to be eradi-
cated; just keep them chained up. The problem is in
compromising one's potential hostility and aggressiveness
so that they are kept just under that dangerous boiling
point where explosions are most apt to occur. This will
cause tensions to build within you—no doubt about it—but
the solution lies elsewhere. You must be able to let these
tensions out in other ways so that they will not be harmful,
and you must be able to empathize by putting yourself in
the other fellow's shoes as often as possible. This brings us
to our fourth key to success in the climb to leadership:
*Learn how to communicate effectively, and learn how to
exercise your power by healthy, nondestructive means of
communication.*

SUMMARY

Power is both awesome and illusory. It is a dangerous
instrument that must be used carefully, and the only way

that we can use it is to understand what the power to lead others consists of, what limitations are placed on power, and what responsibilities the holder of power has to those around him.

Gaining power by devious methods is not advisable. What we must carefully guard against is associating with those kinds of people in our organization who use unsavory techniques as shortcuts to power. Choose your associates and friends wisely. Stay away from the unhappy neurotics who will surely hinder your progress toward the top if you let them get in your way.

Teamwork is essential to the success of any organization, but it also means the sharing of power. Understand the various methods of sharing power, and what risks and benefits each method carries with it, so that you can become an intelligent wielder of power when your turn comes.

Crisis management presents both a challenge and an opportunity. It is a challenge to your acumen and preparation for the various crises that your organization will face; it is also an opportunity for you to show your "stuff" and be able to leapfrog your advancement into the leadership. So welcome crisis for the opportunity that it really is.

Communications is the means by which power is exercised. The better the communications, the more facile will be the transmission of power. Your task is to become more expert in communications, since a well-developed network can mean much to the success of your organization (and to you). Communications as a means of expressing power, giving orders, etc. must be a carefully thought out process. Since power is defined as controlled aggression, we must be careful not to *lose* control so that we may get the most cooperation possible from those around us.

The Four Keys to Power

1. Choose the right associates.
2. Choose the best mode of organization.

3. Study and prepare for crisis.
4. Improve your skills of communication.

EXERCISES FOR CHAPTER 1

1. *Self-control*
Before you can have power over others, you must first be able to demonstrate that you have power (self-control) over yourself. Self-control is the distinguishing hallmark of the successful executive. To develop that necessary self-control, undertake one or more of the following suggestions:

(a) Take up and master a sport (jogging, racquetball, swimming, bicycling, tennis, etc.) if you are physically able.
(b) Give up smoking. Be sure to set a goal.
(c) Go on a diet. Set a goal.
(d) Learn a new skill.

Whatever you want to do, set your mind to accomplish that task within a given period of time (2 weeks, 2 months, etc.) and carefully keep a record of your progress, so that you can see the results for yourself.

2. *Observation*
Keep a diary or a journal of your daily activities. Make sure that *no one* else sees it. Record your observations of each day at the office, the various problems that arose, and how each was handled, etc. At the end of each week, make a summary and write up your observations and analyses. Then take the same set of events, and work out the solutions that *you* would have applied had you been the person in charge. Do this every week, and you will soon be amazed at how much insight you will develop into the problems of management.

3. *Preparation*
Select a particular problem that your organization may be facing. Prepare a plan of action that can be put into effect when a crisis erupts. Compare your plan to the way in which things were handled. Do this for several months,

and you'll soon be able to analyze the best ways to handle various crisis situations.

NOTES

1. Niccolo Machiavelli, *The Prince and The Discourses.* The Modern Library, New York, 1950, p. 65.

2. "If" by Rudyard Kipling, in *A Kipling Pageant.* The Literary Guild, New York, 1935. pp. 708–709.

2

Luck

Before beginning this chapter, take a piece of paper and write your definition of luck on it. Now put it away, and don't take it out again until you have finished this chapter.

Very early one morning, while having coffee in a small restaurant on the Maine seacoast, I overheard a weather-beaten lobsterman say aloud, "Let's see if ma horoscope says ah'm gonna be a winnuh or a losuh today." That grizzled lobsterman had much in common with many of the kings, presidents, dictators, and other powerful people in history. Many of us read our daily horoscopes in the morning newspapers trying to gain some clue as to what lies in store for us. The belief that our destinies are guided by unseen forces that we cannot understand has dominated the activities of human beings since time began. Most of us have our lucky days, our lucky numbers, four-leaf clovers, rabbits' feet, etc. In many cultures, it is still considered important to consult an astrologer before getting married or entering into a business deal.

Few of us ever stop to analyze what we mean by luck—good or bad. In fact, you probably had great trouble coming to grips with any definition at all. Most define luck, as does Webster's Dictionary, as "a force that brings good fortune or adversity." Yet for a person who is motivated to rise to the top, luck becomes a factor in his thinking. "What kind of luck will pursue me?" becomes an important question indeed. When we hear of the misfortune of others, we usually comment, "Tough break for Joe." Thus, Joe's tough break is translated into the notion that Joe has suffered a streak of bad luck. Conversely, when someone has had success, we comment, "Joe sure is lucky." Yet, few of us ever take the time and energy to analyze what we mean by luck, or question whether or not we can do anything about our luck. Can we change bad luck to good luck? Are there such things as "born losers" or people who were born under "lucky stars?"

Despite all of the sophistication and learning of the present era, people still cling to a belief in luck. Fortunes are still being risked on hunches or on a throw of the dice. The amount of money spent in this country on gambling is staggering. People wouldn't gamble so much if they didn't believe in luck. But one interesting fact is that the more one gambles, i.e. becomes a compulsive gambler, the less likely he is to become a winner in the long run. Why is this so? Because one of the symptoms of the compulsive gambler is that of blind faith that he will "luck out." The gambler rarely knows when to quit, and succeeds only in losing everything that he has. Compulsive gamblers pay little attention to reality; they just hope that Lady Luck will bestow her favors on them. One of the remarkable things about compulsive gamblers is that they do not have any systematic approach to their gambling. Why? Because they do not believe that human will or human intervention plays any role at all in their "luck." But if they would reflect for a moment, they would realize that simply their voluntary act of going to the place where they gamble is an act of will; hence, they must have something to do with their luck—good or bad. Obviously, the notion of staking everything one has on a throw of the dice is a notion that does not hold much appeal for the average rational person. Yet, many of us continue to cling to our superstitions and belief in luck.

One of the chief reasons for this continued belief that luck can guide our destinies is the fact that there are large numbers of people who seem to lead charmed lives. They get all the good jobs and promotions; nothing they do produces any misfortune for them. Hence, we all become convinced that if good fortune always visits these people, then there must be such a force. On the other side of the coin, we also see people who never make out. They always get the worst of jobs; they're never promoted although everyone agrees that they are deserving. They end their lives on the treadmill of oblivion. Fame and fortune never give any of them so much as a first glance. So there seems to be some strong evidence that there is such a thing as fortune or luck and we are tempted to disagree with Shakespeare, "The fault, dear Brutus, is not in our stars, But in ourselves that we are underlings."[1] Thus, we acquire a belief early in life that our destinies are somehow guided. Many of us strive to control the forces that guide these destinies, but give up in frustration.

There is an old proverb that goes, "Wise men dream at night, fools both day and night." It is indeed a fool's folly to believe that luck is blind, or that good or bad luck will come to us strictly as a matter of chance. Many studies have been made in recent years that indicate that luck is not as blind or as chancy as we think. Indeed, there are growing indications that people who seemingly enjoy good luck in their careers and lives have a lot to do with directing good fortune their way by the manner in which they conduct their conscious activities. In fact, the studies of successful executives, artists, and professional people, indicate that many of those who were successful in life had a great deal to do with steering Lady Luck in their direction. And most of them agree that luck played an important role in their successful careers, although few of them can explain why they were lucky.

In *your* climb to the top, luck will play an important role. Although good luck can sometimes be as elusive and as slippery as trying to grab a goldfish in a goldfish bowl, you should not despair. There is much that we can do to enhance our luck, but first we must learn the fine art of caution and analysis. For it is precisely at those moments when everything is going our way and we are feeling lucky that Lady Luck in her fickleness will leave us— when our guard is down and we least expect that events will take a bad turn for us. There are a number of factors that help to determine what kind of luck we shall probably enjoy in the course of our careers.

The Challenge of Change

Have you ever considered challenging your luck? If not, consider the fact that a person's luck is subject to rapid change—if he is willing to take a chance and use it. The basic problem is that we are not always cognizant when a rapid change in our luck has occurred or is in the process of taking place. Thus, we don't know what to do about it, and we are generally unprepared to do anything about it when it is apparent that our luck is changing for the better. The reason that we so often fumble our luck is that we don't understand when it is pulling us along and when it is not; nor are we generally capable of synchronizing our activities with changes in our luck. If we are to make any sense out of what appears to be blind luck, we must approach the problem systematically and rigorously. The problem of understanding luck must be attacked from five different points of view. These five points of view are:

1. Confluence
2. Risking
3. Network
4. Preserving
5. Worrying

Let us take each of these factors, one at a time, and try to understand the role that each can play in our rise to the top.

Confluence

Almost everyone experiences at one time or another during his life what I would call "the magic moment." This magic moment is that time when all seems to fall into place, when several good things seem to be happening for you at once. It may be a time when you are falling in love, getting a pat on the back from the boss, or getting a promotion, etc. What is significant about the magic moment is that several other nice things seem to be happening at the same time as well. Why? Because your outlook and optimism are changing at the same time as the magic moment, and you are causing a radiation effect. Good vibrations are flowing from you and are being reflected back to you. Thus, in a spirit of high optimism and good feelings, everything and everyone about you is a receptor and a reflector of good things. This is the magic moment. Why? Because it only lasts for a short time, and the good feelings associated with it are never explained

Magic moments also represent what we call confluence. This is a point at which a number of conditions or events come together that will produce the magic moment. The trouble is, we don't easily recognize the confluence of events or conditions at the time that they are taking place.

There are other factors at work that help to explain confluence, and how we can recognize it. Many famous mathematicians and scientists have tried to reckon with the problem of confluence. Such men have given this problem a number of different labels such as synchronicity (C. G. Jung), seriality (Pascal), clustering, or coincidence. All of these theories are an attempt to explain confluence—why things happen in clusters, or why events happen together. For example, you are walking down the street. You meet an old friend whom you haven't seen for a year. You chat a few moments and then take your leave. A few minutes later while continuing down the street, you meet another friend whom you haven't seen for a long time. Here, on a crowded street, you have met, within 15 minutes, two old friends. You could go for weeks, perhaps months, without seeing anyone you knew, yet within a few moments, you have seen two old friends. This is a simple example of clustering or confluence, but it will serve to illustrate the point that for some unexplained reason things seem to happen in bunches and when we least expect them. Some scientists and philosophers have reasoned that there are forces that cause coincidences to happen that we do not understand; their main point, however, is that the universe is a well-ordered place, and that the repetition of events as well as the creation of coincidences are part of the plan; and we poor mortals are simply not omniscient or perceptive enough to be able to predict when and where these happenings will take place.

If good luck can be said to come in bunches, so does bad luck. A famous French mathematician, René Thom, developed a catastrophe theory sometime in the 1960s. In it, he explained why major disasters such as wars, stock market crashes, etc. take place. Thom's analysis depends on confluence. That is, a number of unfavorable factors coming together at the same time and following a course from which there is no easy return. The result—about the same as falling off a cliff. There is no easy way of picking yourself up and putting yourself back together again once you have fallen off the edge. The moral of Thom's theory is: Don't allow bad luck to pile up on you, or you are facing a catastrophe. Bunches of bad luck are not merely accidents. They are bunches of bad decisions, bunches of bad friends and associates, or even bunches of bad jobs. If we accept the idea that good—and bad—things will happen to us in bunches or clusters, then it makes sense for us to develop some sensitivity to the events around us and to become better interpreters of what those events mean to us. Conversely, we must carefully weigh our actions and decisions so that they will exert the greatest influence possible in "piling up" bunches of good developments.

The chief lesson to be learned from the theory of confluence is that there is no "single" event in our life—rather a series of events that we must be cognizant of, that will predict our successes and failures. We must learn to profit by our successes and realize that they are not going to last forever. We must learn to realize when events are clustering against us and be able to accept them (roll with the punches) while looking for the cluster of events that will signal a change. This is not easy to do and will take careful thought and analysis on your part; but reflection on the events in your organization, for example, will begin to make you more sensitive and perceptive. This brings us to the first rule in making our own luck: *Accept the idea that good things happen in bunches. Learn to recognize these good things and to stretch your luck when they are happening—remember the magic moment. Conversely, learn to be cautious when bad things are happening. Remember the catastrophe theory.*

Risking

Should I change my job? Should I tell the boss the truth? Should I apply for that new position? All these are risks, because they could mean failure as well as success. Yet, if we never took any chances in life, we'd still be on the treadmill to nowhere. One of the key elements in making our luck is the element of risk. We must know when, where, why, and under what conditions we can take the risks that may lead to the top. Obviously, taking chances is not an easy thing to do. Therefore, it would be fruitful to look at risk taking and try to analyze why people take chances, and then we can learn how you can apply some of these reasons to your own behavior, so that when you decide to take a chance, you will be taking it with the best possible odds in your favor.

Why do people take chances? Why do they suddenly change life styles or jobs and depart for the uncertain life that they have chosen rather than remain in the security that they know? A college president I know regularly changes his job every 5 years. He explains his risk taking as adventures into the unknown, without which there would be very little stimulation or challenge for him. He feels that he would grow "stale" on the job, and lose his effectiveness if he stayed longer than 5 years. For most of us, changing jobs every 5 years would be mortifying. Yet, this college president thrives on it. He has learned to live with his risk taking and even to enjoy it.

If you are ever going to reach the top, part of your luck will certainly be the amount of risk that you are willing to take. Remember the adage, "Behold the turtle—he only makes progress when he sticks his neck out?" Taking chances will have to become second nature to you, so if you're not used to taking them, you should stop and take the time to analyze the reasons that we take chances. Some of these are very bad reasons and can lead to disastrous results. Others are very good reasons, and will constructively enhance our decision to build a new image and a new career.

There are four basic reasons why we take chances. These are: Esteem, control, growth, and change. Each of these reasons has a lot to do with our luck. Whether we will make it to the top of the heap has a lot to do with how we handle risks and why we undertake them in the first place. Let's look at each factor in turn.

Much of what we do in life is for esteem. Sometimes, it's for self-esteem, so that we can have a good image of ourselves; at other times, it is so that we can make a good impression on those around us. It is frequently important to us to achieve a better job, not for the money, but because it will raise our esteem in the eyes of those who love us. But frequently, we take chances that we think will improve our esteem for the wrong reasons as well. We may want to use our new position to reward our egos, not to know and meet new challenges. "If only I were the boss, then they'd all have to show me some respect" . . . might be the irrational reasoning in our subconscious. We may never be aware, in fact, that the reasons for our risk taking may be simply the byproduct of a childish kind of egotism. Or we might want to show a critical relative or parent that we really do have the stuff to be a good executive, etc. These are also bad and irrational reasons for taking risks with your career. To be sure, risk taking for reasons of raising one's esteem is rational and valid, but before you engage in changing jobs, moving up the ladder, etc. you should be careful to analyze the reasons that you are seeking to improve your status. Make sure they are constructive reasons based on a rational desire to enhance your image, not because you want to show someone else that they had the wrong perception of you or that you are just as good as they are. In other words, esteem must be seen as ego-building, *not* as ego-rewarding. So if you're going to put yourself on the line and ask to be made head of the department that's in so much trouble, do it for the right reason—to prove to *yourself* that you can do it successfully. Remember, you don't have anything to prove to anyone else except you. Raise your self-esteem and the world will recognize you. You won't have to broadcast the good news to anyone.

Similarly, people take chances because they want to assert control—control over themselves, control over others. Again, risk taking for the sake of taking control is worthy, but one must be cognizant of the reasons. There are those people who will not surrender control for the most irrational of reasons—they are afraid that they will lose control of themselves. An executive I knew would never delegate any authority, and consequently never took any vacations or time off from his job. He was afraid that he would be surrendering control once someone else knew the inside secrets of his job. The result was a nervous wreck of an executive who became overworked, irritable, and quite thoroughly disliked by his peers. Our reasons for wanting to take control must be, therefore, quite rational. We must want to take risks because we feel that we are ready and capable of exercising control over others at the time. Before you can control others, you must first demonstrate that you can control yourself. That is, be able to prove that you are an inner-directed person who can plan and organize. Then you will be at the point that you can exercise control over others. To take a risk that involves directing others or assuming large responsibilities before you are ready for them is an invitation to disaster. So if you're going to be risking yourself to gain control, ask yourself the reasons why. Analyze your need to control, and be sure that it is a rational need before you move into such responsibility.

Another reason for taking risks is that of growth. If we never take chances, we never grow. Growth implies taking on more responsibilities as well as taking on the risks of defeat and failure. Growth, therefore, implies that we are willing to risk loss in order to achieve something higher or better than we now have. It has often been said that we learn nothing from success; we learn much from failure. Growing is precisely that—risking failure as well as success. Indeed, most successful people believe that taking risks and failing has been the greatest education that they've ever had. To grow is to learn, and whether we succeed or fail is not as important as the learning that occurs as a result.

Risking in order to grow also means that we have to come to terms with ourselves as well. We must face our shortcomings as well as our virtues and be able to be thoroughly honest about them. We must be willing to accept the personal responsibility for our failures and not blame the rest of the world. When you are ready to concede that your success or failure is your own responsibility, not someone else's, then you're ready to take the risks that lead to growth.

In one sense, growing means burning your bridges behind you. Once you have made the decision to grow, there should be no consideration of retrogression. You have now decided to make the great leap across the chasm that separates you from the world of achievement, and it is essential that you have the attitude that there will be no turning back once this decision has been made. It is irrevocable. Having taken the kind of stance, you will be surprised at how determined you are to succeed.

Many famous and well-known people have gotten where

they are as a simple act of defiance. The famous trial lawyer, F. Lee Bailey, for example, pointed out that whenever
someone tells him that he can't do something, he gets his
back up and becomes defiant. Growing is an act of defiance
because you're attempting to do something that your
friends and relatives tell you that you can't do. So become
an achiever, and be ready to make that great leap into a
new dimension. "But am I ready for it?" you may ask.
Primarily, that is a question you alone must answer. If you
have been giving any consideration to the thought of growing, chances are, you are ready. The exercises at the end
of this chapter may be very helpful in determining
whether or not you are ready. Always remember, however,
that even if the great leap results in what appears to be
failure, you have grown, and it is not failure if you have
learned from the experience. George B., a young junior
executive, decided that he was ready for a try at being vice
president in charge of sales. He applied to a smaller company than the one he was working for, but found that it
made demands on his skills and talents too great for him
at the time. George learned by his experiences what was
demanded of a vice president at that level, and although
he had to retreat temporarily to a lower level job, he was
still much better prepared than most of his contemporaries. So if you adopt the attitude that all of your experiences
are a school, not a final degree, you will find yourself growing at a more rapid rate than you ever dreamed possible.

Finally, risking means change. To take a chance means
that you must be contemplating change for yourself. This
means the kind of change that will revolutionize your
thinking and your outlook. Some call it possibility thinking, others call it positive thinking, but by whatever name
or label we call it, taking the risk of changing your attitude
can be the bravest thing you'll ever do. Change also dem-
onstrates that you are capable of learning and applying
the lessons learned to yourself. Harry S. graduated from
one of the most prestigious graduate schools of business
administration in the United States. He got a job with a
major corporation as a junior executive. Within a year,

however, Harry was fired. The reason? He was too abrasive—he did not get along well with his colleagues. What was Harry's response to the problem? He began psychological counseling to find out why he was so abrasive with people and how he could overcome these destructive tendencies. Harry certainly had the ability to do his job well; he lacked the personality characteristics, but was willing to take the risks involved to make the basic changes that were required. It is not easy to make the kind of sacrifices that basic change requires. Moreover, one is risking a way of life that has become comfortable. That is why giving up bad habits is so difficult. But as Harry learned, one must accept the risk of change because the world will not accommodate itself to you, and the organizational world is especially demanding in this regard.

Taking risks is a way of changing our luck. We cannot change our luck unless we are ready and willing to gamble. But risk taking need not be a blind or senseless gamble. We are not depending on capricious Lady Luck to bestow her favors on us. Rather, we are determinedly surveying the odds and prudently gauging our readiness to take the risks that are involved in making it to the top. Moreover, we are ready to assume the costs that risk taking involves, and we are ready to live with the results— good or bad. This brings us to the second rule in making our own luck: *To enhance your luck, you must be willing to take risks. That is, give up something you have for something that you hope to obtain. Such risks must be minimized by intelligent consideration of the factors involved, if they are to be successful.*

Network

The next key to enticing Lady Luck to sit in our corner instead of the other person's is that of establishing a new series of connections for ourselves. The reason that many men and women are successful in reaching the top echelon is not just talent. There are many talented people who never become successful in the quest for leadership because these unfortunates have consistently kept their talents to themselves, and they have never played a role in establishing their own network.

What do we mean by a network? Visualize a fisherman who casts out his nets upon the water. He drags in a great many valuable things that he wants in his nets (fish) as well as many things that he doesn't want (seaweed, debris). In a sense, you are that fisherman, casting out your net as far and as wide as possible in the hope that you'll catch a lot of good fish (contacts) as well as some useless debris. Even that useless debris can turn out to be a valuable catch. A chance meeting or a chance word can lead to opportunity for you. When someone you know seems to enjoy success in obtaining jobs or promotions, haven't you heard others frequently remark, "Lucky Joe—he's got contacts!" ? Joe wasn't lucky—he was smart because he knew that the successful fisherman isn't going to catch any fish unless he casts out his nets. When executive recruiters (better known as "headhunters" in the trade) go looking for talented people, they usually ask for referrals from someone whose opinion they respect. Unless your net has been cast out, you're likely to be overlooked. You can be the most talented and capable person in the world, but if your circle is small, few will know about you. If your circle is large, your chances of coming to the attention of others will be considerably enhanced.

How does one go about widening this circle? One young executive, Richard B., often traveled for his company. On the plane, he always made it a habit to strike up a conversation with his fellow passenger. The result? A number of excellent job offers came his way as a result of these chance encounters. If he had sat in his seat with his nose buried in a magazine, no opportunities would have come his way. Another young government bureaucrat, Edward S., made it his business to join and attend all of the various professional organizations that he could. He even held an office or two in some of them. A number of job offers, one of them involving a considerable promotion to head of a new agency, came to him as a result. Whether it's joining professional organizations or meeting strangers while traveling, or becoming active in your community orga- nizations (another excellent way of meeting people), it is imperative for your advancement that you cast out the biggest net possible. Remember, good and talented people are *always* a rare commodity, and there's always someone searching for just the kind of person that you might be. He'll never meet you, however, if you keep to yourself. This brings us to the third rule for improving our luck: *Make the largest number of contacts—business, social, professional—that you can. The key to discovery is expo- sure.*

Preserving

How can we retain the good luck that we have acquired? Or, to put it another way, can we stretch our luck? There are many who believe we can. For the most part, preserv- ing good luck means keeping bad luck away from our door. As we have already seen, most bad luck comes to us in the form of bad judgment. We choose the wrong job, the wrong associates, etc. Thus, bad luck is bound to become our con- stant companion. So a bit of foresight and intuition are necessary to keep misfortune from our door. Consider, for example, the case of the late Joseph P. Kennedy. As a Wall Street speculator in 1929, the late Joe Kennedy had a great deal of money invested in a Bull Market that it seemed would continue rising forever. One early fall day he was having his shoes shined in the Wall Street district, and the shoeshine boy was telling him how rapidly the market was rising and how he, the shoeshine boy was rapidly gaining a fortune—all on paper, of course. As Joe Kennedy later told his friends, "If that shoeshine boy claimed to be as smart as I was, I figured one of us was wrong—and it was time for me to get out of the market." Joe Kennedy withdrew from the stock market just in time to avoid the great crash of October, 1929 that ruined thousands of "smart" people. There are hundreds of similar stories, all with the same point to make. That is, preserving one's good fortune is largely a matter of intelligence and fore-sight. If we are suffering from a run of bad luck, it is time for us to reconsider our moves as well as our thinking. Perhaps we are stuck in the wrong job. Time to change? People who continue to stumble from one bad job to another are not seriously or intelligently studying their options. Similarly, people who are stuck in a job that offers them no future are simply doing their best to preserve their bad luck.

Preserving good luck involves a great deal of deliberate and conscious activity on your part. It involves making a plan for yourself and sticking to that plan. Jim B., a young junior executive, has a great deal of ability. He is on the way up, and he does not intend to become stuck in a dead-end job. Therefore, Jim B. has a plan, and sticks to it—if he's not moving up the corporate ladder in 3 years, it's time to be moving on. In this way, Jim B. is stretching his luck by continuing to move laterally, until he does receive the recognition that he feels he deserves. Most successful people have adopted some kind of a plan for themselves. They realize that good luck as well as bad luck comes in bunches, and they have devised a plan for retaining as much of that good luck as possible. The fourth rule, then, for preserving our good luck and staving off the bad is: *Adopt a long-range plan for yourself and stick with it! Build the plan around the idea of minimal risk and preserving the gains that you have already made in life.*

Worrying

At this writing, a major U.S. toy manufacturer has marketed a Christmas toy product that has resulted in the death of several children; a major tire manufacturer has had to recall millions of faulty tires; automobile manufacturers are constantly having to recall their products for flaws, and one company has been sued for the accidental deaths of its customers. What went wrong? Someone didn't worry enough about Murphy's Law: "If anything can go wrong, it will."

Much of what we have won in life is emphemeral and temporary. This includes major corporations that find themselves in a great deal of trouble all of a sudden, as well as individuals like ourselves who fail to realize that the merry-go-round will not continue forever. Constant vigilance is the price of continued success, and those who forget this maxim are bound to pay a heavier price than those who remember it.

It has often been said that lucky people are cautious and pessimistic by nature. A Chinese friend of mine once told me it is a custom among many of his friends who own successful restaurants to constantly complain that business is "lousy" even though their restaurants are crowded with diners night after night. These successful men are simply stating their belief that the worst can happen at any moment and to gloat over their good fortune is to invite a swift kick in the rear from Lady Luck. People—and organizations—that enjoy good luck worry about it. They have not only made contingency plans for when things go wrong, but they face the future with just enough pessimism and skepticism to prepare themselves for Murphy's Law. Whether or not bad fortune comes to us as a matter of outside forces and events over which we have no control (independent variables—those things that affect us, but over which we have no direct control), or whether bad fortune comes to us from our own misdirected efforts and lack of intelligence (dependent variables—those things that *we* can change and have some control over), makes little difference. The main point to remember is that our luck, flighty and capricious as it might be, depends to a great extent on our vigilance; and vigilance, it turns out, is nothing more than a synonym for worrying. Thus, our fifth rule for providing ourselves with good luck is: *Be constantly vigilant. Worry about the things that seem "safe" or "sure"—those are the things that are bound to go wrong. Remember Murphy's Law.*

REVIEW THE PAST

A recent sampling of Harvard College graduates who responded to a questionnaire indicated that 25 years after they graduated, more than 50 percent of them are doing something in life different from what they had expected to do. In fact, most people end up in different occupations and vocations than they had planned on pursuing when they were young. The chief lesson behind these facts is that unplanned twists and turns in the road of life have a lot more to do with our luck than we would like to admit. Many more people have stumbled into their present vocations by accident than by design.

George Santayana once wrote, "Those who cannot remember the past are condemned to repeat it,"[2] and although you cannot do anything about your past, it will definitely play a role in planning your future, if you allow it to. One of the basic elements in bringing Lady Luck on our side is to review our past performances and to constantly keep in mind the experiences and trials that we have had in the past. Wisdom is bought only at great cost —the cost and trials of experience. How quickly we would like to forget the unpleasant experiences of the past and forge ahead to new delights, but the past must always be with us if we do not want to make the same mistakes again.

How can we learn from the past? One simple way is to keep a diary, a journal of our past experiences. If this is something that you have neglected to do, why not start now? It can be a record of your victories as well as your mistakes and defeats, but from it you can learn what you did right as well as the things that you did that were injurious to your interests. Such a diary or journal can be daily or weekly; it will enable you to analyze your performance at work and to digest the things that have happened to you. Unless we record our reactions and activities, we cannot properly assess the kind of impact that we are having on those around us. Thus, we will be selling ourselves short and not giving luck a chance to operate as effectively as possible on our behalf. We study our past to avoid the costly mistakes that may have postponed our progress. For the same reason, corporations issue quarterly reports, organizations issue progress reports, and students of military strategy study the great battles of the past; for indeed, what is past is prologue. Below is an example of what a journal or diary might look like:

WEEK OF   December 10th
_____

Accomplishments
1. Was able to resolve the crisis over certain supplies by getting to the right person in the shipping department. Perseverence pays!
2. Made a suggestion for a new filing system—hope it will be adopted. If not, I believe that I didn't make a strong enough case.
3. I was able to resolve a dispute between Joan and Annette. Those two just don't like each other at all, so I'll have to accept the role of peacemaker. Anyway, I was able to rescue this one by having them take turns answering the telephone.

Obstacles
1. Unable to persuade the boss to change our supplier. I used too much pressure, and not enough reason. Next time I must be more persuasive and use less "strong-arm" tactics.
2. I ignored Jack in the hallway. *Must not do that again!* Jack is mighty sensitive these days. Can't afford not to have him on my side.

Summary for the Week
Be more persuasive, less argumentive. Keep the peace between Joan and Annette. Don't forget to maintain contact, even if the other fellow doesn't see you.

Such a journal as illustrated above can be of tremendous help in "loading up" your gun because it will enable you to see your mistakes, and mistakes are—let's face it—what make bad luck worse. Memory misrepresents the past; keeping a journal will keep you closer to reality and enable you to see why and even how you made certain decisions, such as taking on a new job or responsibility. Thus, you can do a great deal to analyze your past as well as plan your future. Good luck will come only to those who prepare for it, and understanding how and why we behave as we do is one of the keys to making luck work *for* us. Our sixth rule, then, is: *Keep a diary or journal of your accomplishments as well as your failures and obstacles. Try to analyze why you were successful or unsuccessful and learn to avoid unsuccessful behavior.*

MAKE A WISH

Wishes have been described as the dreams of youth and the frustrations of old age. Yet, wishing becomes an important part of life—and of luck. For if we never wished, we'd never try. Wishing won't make it so, but it will make it possible. If wishing can be said to be the child of despair, it can also be said to be the father of desire. And it is desire that goads us on in life. Never to dream, never to try, is never to win.

What has wishing got to do with your luck in reaching the top? For one thing, if you don't wish, you don't *want,* and wanting is one of the keys to success. It has often been said that hopelessness and/or helplessness lead to feelings of depression. The only way to counteract such feelings is to wish for change, and then a strange question enters your mind. *"Why not?"* becomes the strange new question that fills your mind instead of the depressive thinking that has had you in its chains heretofore. As we have said earlier, luck is lying around in the street, waiting to be picked up. Wishing—wanting—to change your luck becomes the first step in a positive direction. Don't be afraid to dream of what seems to be the impossible. In fact, the one great quality that all leaders have in common is the ability to have vision, to be able to dream of the impossible, to see ahead. Great enterprises were built by men with only a vision—and very little else. Their many stories are too well known to be repeated here, but the one common wish that they all shared was the wish to *become number one!* And that wish saw them through. As Arthur O'Shaughnessy wrote:

> One man with a dream, at pleasure, Shall go forth and conquer a crown.[3]

Remember, you cannot become lucky unless you *wish* to. That's the first step.

THE NATURE—AND POWER—OF POSITIVE THINKING

Positive thinking is the most powerful drug that there is. Many scientists today have confirmed that beneficial changes occur in people who engage in this kind of thinking. There are said to be links between the body's biochemistry and the benefits of optimistic thinking. Believing that all things are possible will be another important step in changing your luck. In fact, there are four traits that are keys to positive thinking. These can be best remembered by the acronym, ECCO: Enthusiasm, courage, confidence, and optimism. Have the enthusiasm to reach for the top, and you will. Have the courage to dare to become the best, and you will. Have the confidence to know that you *are* the best, and you will be the best. Have the optimism that good luck will become your campaign manager, and it will.

Lucky people, as we have found, tend to be people who think and plan, but they are also people who subscribe to the idea that without enthusiasm for what they're doing, the courage to do it, the confidence in their ability to do it, and the optimism that they're going to succeed, their thinking and planning would all be for nothing. To change *your* luck, begin to think positively. Never say maybe or perhaps or cannot. Instead, make your brain say, "Why not?"—and it will!

When we first began this chapter, I asked you to write your definition of luck on a piece of paper, and then put it

away. Now take it out and read it. Surprised? Probably you
are because by now you have come to realize that there is
much more to luck than blind chance. Each person, by his
or her own efforts, can enhance or diminish his or her
luck. Always remember that you are as lucky as you make
yourself. Good luck!

SUMMARY

Most of us have been conditioned to believe that good or
bad luck depends on mysterious forces beyond our ability
to control; yet a little serious reflection on the role that we
can play in enhancing our own luck rapidly leads us to the
conclusion that we have more to do with making our own
luck than we think. Nevertheless, luck remains elusive
and must be conserved carefully by us.

The work of many scholars and philosophers has led us
to believe that there are five factors that have a great deal
to do with the kind of luck that we will enjoy during our
lifetimes. These factors are: *Confluence,* when a series of
important factors converge to make our lives change direction; *risking,* which means that we should not be afraid
to take risks at the right time and under the right conditions; *network*, which means that we should strive at all
times to enlarge our circle of acquaintances because they
will become the source for our future opportunities; *preserving* means holding the good luck that you have already achieved by being conservative and prudent;
worrying means that you should never let your guard
down at any time. Lady Luck is fickle and can desert you
without warning. People who are lucky are people who
worry, and that is what keeps them striving.

One sure way for us to prepare for the future is to review
our past. We can best do this by keeping a journal or a
diary of our daily experiences and reflections, and this
will be a great aid in helping us to perceive the reality of
our activities much more clearly.

We should not underestimate the role that is played by wishing. It gives us desire and goads us on to achieve incredible heights. Similarly, positive thinking plays a very important role in our lives. Without the qualities of enthusiasm, courage, confidence, and optimism, we would not become successful no matter how much good fortune might come our way. So a positive attitude is quite necessary as a catalyst to speed up and take advantage of lucky events or magic moments.

THE SIX RULES FOR BECOMING LUCKY

1. Accept the idea that good things happen in bunches. Learn to recognize these good things, and to stretch your luck when they are happening—remember the magic moment! Conversely, learn to be cautious when bad things are happening to you. Remember the catastrophe theory.
2. To enhance your luck, you must be willing to take risks. That is, give up something you have for something that you hope to obtain. Such risks must be minimized by intelligent consideration of the factors involved, if they are to be successful.
3. Make the largest number of contacts—business, social, and professional—that you can. The key to the discovery of your *unique* talents is exposure.
4. Adopt a long-range plan for yourself and stick with it! Build the plan around the idea of minimal risk and preserving the gains that you have already made in life.
5. Be constantly vigilant. Worry about things that seem "safe" or "sure"—those are the things that are bound to go wrong. Remember Murphy's Law.
6. Keep a diary or journal of your accomplishments as well as your failures and obstacles. Try to analyze why you were successful or unsuccessful, and learn to avoid unsuccessful behavior.

EXERCISES FOR CHAPTER 2

1. Network

Take a sheet of paper and make two columns. The first column should be headed, "business"; the second column should be headed "social." Now under each column list *all* the friends and acquaintances that you have. Try to do this in chronological order. Next step: List all the new friends and acquaintances that you made during the past year. Have you made at least five new acquaintances? No? Then take 10 percent of the total business and social acquaintances that you have made during your life. If you have made 50, 10 percent will result in five. That is your goal for the coming year—five new acquaintances to be made during the year. Keep a record of these new acquaintances, and resolve to add 10 percent each year. You'll be amazed at how fast your circle of influence will continue to grow if you use this method. You may, if you wish, "cheat" a little by renewing an old friendship or acquaintance—someone you haven't seen for more than 3 years.

2. Chancing it

During this year, read the biographies of at least five people who have made a great success of their lives. Examples: Henry Ford, Thomas Edison, Alfred Sloan. Take notes on how many times they took risks in their careers, and find out if these risks paid off. Examine the lives of these well-known people to determine if there is any pattern. That is, under what circumstances did they decide to take risks? You'll be surprised at the answer—when they were sure of themselves and sure of what they were doing. You'll also be surprised to find out that few of these people paid any attention to economic conditions, prophesies of gloom or doom, or anything else, once they were *sure* of what they were doing and, of course, sure of their ability to do it.

3. Wishing

On a piece of paper, write down your expectations—where you'd like to be and what you'd like to be doing: (a) in 5 years; (b) in 10 years; (c) in 15 years. Now that you know what you want to be, you can get busy achieving your wishes—and that will be 50 percent of your good luck!

NOTES

1. William Shakespeare, *Julius Caesar,* Act I, sc. iii.

2. George Santayana, *The Life of Reason.* Charles Scribner's Sons, New York, 1954. p. 82.

3. William Alexander Percy (ed), *Poems of Arthur O'Shaughnessy.* Yale University Press, New Haven, 1923. p. 39.

3

Ability

Top Executives Don't Always Stay on Top

Executive mobility is a fact of life that can provide us
with the opportunity that we are looking for. Few executives stay in the same position for more than 5 years, and
most executives will work for at least four firms before
their careers are over. Even the federal government has
pushed through civil service reforms that allow for room
at the top. These new reforms allow for the firing of in-
competent executives and for the awarding of incentive
bonuses to the competent ones. State and local governments throughout the United States that are looking for
able executives are beginning to sit up and take notice,
and are starting to copy the federal government's break
with tradition. Moreover, as the financial and managerial
problems grow, the hunger for good executive talent
grows with it. Be sure of one thing—competency will reap
rich rewards in the near future because we have learned
the lesson that resources and talent cannot be wasted any
longer. Whether you work for a corporation or a govern-

ment agency, therefore, matters little. There is always going to be room at the top, and that's where you are headed!

Why don't top executives always stay there? Statistics
show that four out of every five of the top executive officers
(comptroller, vice president, and president) of United
States corporations either move up or move out within 10
years. Corporate life represents a winnowing-out process
whereby "only the fittest will survive." For many executives who are unsuccessful at managing one firm, there is
always the lateral route; that is, attempting to move side-
ways and transferring your talents to another firm at the
same level. This strategy has limited value, however, because having a reputation as a "floater" is not very desirable. There are a number of reasons why some top
executives are unsuccessful. It will be instructive for us to
take a look at them.

The first and most important reason is *inflexibility.* The
executive in question has lost his ability to respond to
change. "The twig that will not bend with the wind will
break." This does not mean that every executive must be
such a "yes man" or so wishy-washy that he or she will
agree with everyone, and no one at the same time. What
it *does* mean is that the intelligent executive is one who is
constantly prepared for new conditions and new changes.
Such new developments as new assignments, change in
new products, change in the personnel structure, change
in the people that you work with, or change in the management structure are all shocks to one's nervous system. But
we must be able and ready to respond to these kinds of
challenges, not with a grudging willingness, but with a
sense of excitement for a new challenge. Adaptability is
more than a sign of intelligent survival—it is a sign of
being willing to participate in a challenge to your abilities.

A second reason that some executives don't succeed is
that they are unable to delegate authority properly. Part of
the reason for this failure is that they never learned how
to delegate authority by organizing and assigning tasks to
subordinates. There are two extremes to this problem, and
one is as bad as the other. Either the executive in question

assigns the tasks to his subordinates and then fails to monitor their progress, or he follows them too closely, giving them the idea that they cannot be trusted to perform a simple task. The executive who is "Trusting Tom" is as bad as the executive who is "Nervous Ned." A certain amount of monitoring is quite necessary, but the executive who signals a complete lack of trust in his subordinates is bound to have a morale problem.

A third reason for executive failure is the failure to be able to properly organize the use of time. Time is the only nonrenewable resource that we have. We can replenish energy; we can replenish money; we can replenish hunger or thirst; we can replenish want; but we cannot provide ourselves with a new supply of *time.* Thus, time becomes the one element that has to be guarded more closely than any other in our lives. Waste your time, and you have wasted your most precious resource. Waste the time of your organization, and you have squandered your organization's right to success. There are two major guidelines to the successful use of time. The first is rationing. Time must be rationed if it is to be used intelligently. Rationing means planning ahead and assigning blocks of time to the future. The second guideline is conserving. If we are always conscious of the need to conserve, we are less apt to squander time. Successful executives are keenly aware of the need to make the most out of the limited time that they have. Conversely, unsuccessful people tend to squander their time allotments and give little thought to planning. The old adages of "one day at a time" or "take each day as it comes" will never even be considered by the successful person, for they will leave nothing to chance when it comes to making the best possible use of their time. I know of one executive who runs three companies and writes business articles for a newspaper. How does he do all this? He told me once—by time management. By assigning blocks of time to each of his enterprises, and sticking to it. He even utilized his train commuting time to advantage.

I am reminded of a story that can serve to illustrate the necessity of conserving time. A sales manager was having a session with his salesmen. He had already covered the main points of his presentation, but was going over and over the same material, taking three times as much time as he should have. Finally, one of the desperate salesmen turned to his colleague and said, "Boy, the sales manager sure is wasting a lot of time." His colleague responded, "He's wasted *all* his time—he's now into eternity!" Don't let that happen to you. Make your point and realize that it's time to move on or you're out of time. Experts who have studied the ways in which successful executives operate find that their daily time management patterns are characterized by two major qualities: brevity and frequency. That is, they spend only a short amount of time at each task, and they perform a variety of functions. Obviously, if this is what executives must do, then time management becomes a very important part of our daily lives. So, learn to manage your time well, and you'll avoid one of the major pitfalls that can lead to executive failure.

The fourth reason that executives fail is perhaps the most important—failure to communicate. Communications failure is like a short circuit in an electrical power system. When you cannot make the connection, nothing will happen. One must therefore ask the question, "What is communication?" Here is the answer, and always keep it inscribed in your mind: *Communication is the means whereby the thoughts in my head are transferred to your head.* Sounds simple, doesn't it? Yet, for lack of successful communication, many an organization has failed, and even more executives have failed. Everything that you do, everything that your organization does, is controlled by communications. Failure to communicate adequately also leads to another reason for executive failure—the failure to provide morale.

Emerson was right when he said, "nothing great was ever achieved without enthusiasm."[1] The fifth reason for executive failure is the failure to provide an atmosphere in which there is a high level of morale—enthusiasm for what you are doing. Your enthusiasm can become infectious, and when it is transmitted to those who work below you, you'll have a "swinging" organization. A friend of mine who works for a governmental agency once told me about his "boss." His attitude was that this was a nine to five job, and that he would do nothing creative at all. He was just there to mind the store. This created a different kind of infectious response—the entire agency became so lethargic that the agency became notorious for its failure to produce. Low morale produces a number of diseases that are endemic to an organization on the brink of failure —absenteeism, low productivity, backbiting, slovenliness, and carelessness, to name but a few. The executive who cannot provide enthusiasm cannot therefore have an organization that will succeed. Remember the morale factor. Without it, nothing will move; with it, you can move a mountain.

The first rule, then is: *Executives fail for five important reasons: Inflexibility, inability to delegate authority properly, poor time management, failure to communicate, and failure to be enthusiastic.*

BORN TO RULE?

The temperament necessary to become an executive has often been described as harsh, ruthless, driving, and uncompromising. Again, we are victims of our own fantasies because that is what we think executives ought to be like. If all executives were the ruthless, cruel beings that we thought they should be, then the ulcer and heart attack rate would probably be much higher than it is for the rest of the general population. In fact, it is not. It's much lower, and that goes for the suicide rate as well. One of the things that we're learning about executive behavior is that nice guys don't finish last. So if you consider yourself not to be a good candidate because you're not the ruthless type, take comfort from the fact that most studies have shown executives to be exceptionally well-balanced, considerate individuals who are more interested in creating a good working environment than in browbeating their employees. In fact, hard-driving, ruthless executives are extremely neurotic and make poor managers.

There are seven kinds of abilities that all good executives share. These are:

The ability to decide
The ability to lead
The ability to direct
The ability to communicate
The ability to organize
The ability to plan
The ability to motivate others

Each of these abilities are abilities that can be acquired by you, regardless of your personality, if you are willing to make the effort. Let us look at each ability in turn.

The ability to decide is what most executives are paid for, and because executives are highly paid, the decision-making apparatus in an executive's head is a highly prized piece of machinery. Let's look at this apparatus and see how it makes decisions. The mind makes decisions for its owner on the basis of how well the information received correlates with the perceptions and knowledge of its owner. This is perhaps a long-winded way of saying that if we want to make good decisions, we'd better have plenty of good information before we start.

However, information isn't the only requirement for good decision making. An equally important requirement is the technique that we use in making decisions. There are three basic kinds of techniques: *Rational, incremental, and mixed. Rational* decison making is based upon a choice of alternatives after each alternative has been carefully studied as to its probable outcome. Whenever a rational decision maker decides, therefore, he carefully analyzes all of the costs and all of the benefits that will result from a certain course of action. In this way, he is attempting to use a logical course of action that will produce a predictable result. *Incremental* decision making is partial decision making at best. It puts off as many decisions as possible, and prefers to deal only with the present crisis. This kind of decision making will require much additional decision making, and may even force you to constantly reassess your decisions and continually monitor the effect that they may be having. *Mixed* decision making is one that attempts to keep in mind both the long-term and the short-term effects of the decision that you are making. Now let's take a basic example so that we can better understand how this mental process can be most effectively put to work for you.

You are in charge of obtaining supplies of a certain item that is vital to the production of your company's product. Without these supplies, no production will be possible. There are, however, several options open to you: (1) You could sign a contract with one major supplier, who will guarantee both the price and the delivery, provided that you promise him all of your business. (2) You could decide to remain on the open market and take your chances with price and delivery. (3) You could contract for a guarantee with suppliers for *part* of your needs only, and take your chances for the balance on the open market.

How can we categorize these three types of decisions? If you were to make the first decision, i.e. relying on one supplier, you would fall into the *rational* category because you would be trying to produce a predictable result. If you chose the second answer, you would fall into the *incremental* category because you would be willing to gamble along, making adjustments for price and supply. If you made the third choice, you would be in the *mixed* category because you were not willing to gamble *all* of your supply, even though you could get it at fixed prices. Which of these kinds of decision making are correct? None, because they are all different kinds of reasoning, and may have a lot to do with your personality and the way in which you handle problems. The ability to make decisions, however, means that you must pay attention to the *way* in which you make decisions and be conscious of the techniques that you are using. Perhaps one technique is good at one time, another at another time. The important thing is that you must be aware of the technique that you are using, and then you can begin to question yourself: "Why did I make the decision that I did?" In other words, your ability to decide will improve remarkably when you take a serious look at *how* you decide. Perhaps you'll even decide to use a different technique now and then. As a leader, you'll be paid to decide. Therefore, your decision making must be firm, positive, and based on your personal conviction that it is the best possible decision. It may turn out badly, but you will be faulted less for it if you made it with a technique that you were conscious of.

One final word. Decisions must carry the conviction of the person making them. Do not make an important decision half-heartedly. Only weak leaders do that. Pretend that others are asking you, "Is that what you want to do?" Your firm, unequivocal answer should be "Yes!" Never "maybe" or "perhaps."

The second ability that we categorized was the ability to lead. Let's think for a few moments about what leadership is. Suppose that you were elected or selected to be a leader of others. The first proposition is that you must have followers. That is, there must be people who are willing to follow your direction. Leadership and power are not the same thing because leaders do not control power. Leaders operate on consensus. That is, they have enough people who are willing to follow them. I once spoke with a veteran of World War II who was a member of General George S. Patton's famous tank army. He said, "We loved Patton—we'd have followed him to hell if he asked us to." Why did his men believe in him so much? Because Patton knew where he was going, and his men knew that in following him, they were following someone with purpose and motive. All of the great business and political leaders of this world, whether they were good or bad, attracted followers like flies to honey because their followers sensed that these leaders knew where they were headed and what they wanted to accomplish. The rest—mobilizing their followers—was easy. Most important of all, however, is the observation that all good leaders believe in what they're doing—their conviction that what they're doing is so important or so right, that there are scores of people ready and willing to follow them, in many cases without question.

Perhaps the point that is most important about leaders is that they inspire their followers. One of the best illustrations that I know is contained in Cameron Hawley's novel, *Executive Suite*.[2] The hero of the novel, Don Walling, is in competition with Loren Shaw, the comptroller, for the presidency of a furniture manufacturing corporation. Loren Shaw can only talk to the board about how he will cut costs and improve profits, and thus raise the stockholders' dividends. The board of directors is impressed with his presentation. Then Don Walling takes the floor:

> "I don't want to be facetious about this. . . . Loren's right when he says that we have an obligation to our stockholders—but it's a bigger obligation than just paying dividends. We have to keep this company *alive*. That's the important thing—and a company is like a man. No man can work for money alone. It isn't enough. You starve his soul when you try it—and you can starve a company to death in the same way . . . There was one thing Avery Bullard (the late President) never understood," Don Walling went on, "He never realized that other men had to be proud, too—that the force behind a great company had to be more than the pride of one man—that it had to be the pride of thousands of men. A company is like an army—it fights on its pride."

Then Don Walling, after decrying the cheap products that the men in the furniture factories were being asked to make, says,

> "We haven't even started to grow! Suppose we get fifteen percent of the total—and why not, it's been done in a dozen industries? Fifteen percent and the Tredway Corporation will be five times as big as it is today. All right, I know it hasn't been done before in the furniture business, but does that mean we can't do it? No—because that's exactly what we *are* going to do! . . ." In that last moment, Loren Shaw had suddenly became aware that his brain had been set aflame by a spark from Don

Walling's mind—a spark that he himself could never have supplied. Now he was fired to accomplishments that had been far beyond the limits of his imagination.

Needless to say, Don Walling was elected to the presidency of the corporation by the board of directors because they could see—even his competitor could finally see—that Don Walling knew where he was going and why he was headed there. Most important of all, he was able to kindle a spark—the spark of inspiration among his associates. Now that's leadership!

Finally, what really constitutes excellence in leadership? The following criteria might provide the best answer.

Good leaders:
1. Create and enforce high standards of behavior and accomplishment.
2. Enthuse their followers with the will to succeed and excel.
3. Make their presence felt even when they are not physically present.
4. Recognize achievement; they also know how to provide constructive criticism.

Another important ability for you to develop is the ability to direct others. Directing can best be defined as influencing the actions of those who work under you. In other words, getting people to do your bidding. This may sound easy, but in truth, it's not. In order for you to get your subordinates to accomplish what you want, you must first give them clear, direct, and complete orders. You must tell them: "This is what I want done; this is how I want it done; this is when I want it done." You must be sure that what you want accomplished is within the ability of your subordinates to perform—that is, that they have the means with which to do the job requested. In addition, the employees have to understand what is expected of them, and they must be given a clear signal from you, the boss, that you are either pleased or displeased with the results. Managers motivate employees to accomplish assignments, and thus encourage their subordinates to fulfill the manager's expectations.

In many ways, directing is extremely difficult because of the communications barrier that persists between human beings. Communications, the fourth ability that all good managers must possess, is the other side of the coin. We cannot direct others if we cannot communicate properly with them. Communications is, of course, a two-way street. There is the sender and the receiver. Unless both are part of the transfer of information, the message will be garbled and will fail in its purpose. There are seven major ways of maintaining a good communications set-up in any organization. These are:

1. The channels and the means of communication should be known to all participants. No mysteries please!
2. A definite, formal channel of communication that everyone can recognize. Not a memo scribbled by someone on the back of an old envelope. Yet, it's amazing how many organizations still use the old envelope routine.
3. The lines of communication should be as direct as possible. Get to the point and get to the person that it's intended for.
4. Set up and use a complete communication system. Most organizations should be continually monitoring their communications system, and should keep readjusting it to meet new needs; yet they are not, even though yesterday's methods cannot meet today's needs.
5. The communicators must be competent. That is, those making the communications must be able to do so in such a fashion that they will be received and understood at the other end.
6. Communications should never be interrupted. "Oh, yes," says Sam, "that's for Harry. I'll take it to him."

You'd be amazed at how many times Harry never gets messages. Use a formal, routinized system, and the flow of information will become a lot smoother.

7. Every communication should be signed, dated, and receipted by the receiver. Such a method will save a lot of time and misunderstanding later on.

Recently, an employee of a construction firm was in the field. The firm had a number of different projects on the drawing boards at the architect's office. The employee was telephoning into the construction office to indicate that certain much needed plans for a particular project would be available soon. The employee's cryptic message to his boss' secretary was, "Tell him the drawings are ready." What drawings? When will they be sent? How? All these questions went unanswered, and the boss would simply have to await the drawings to find out if they are the ones that he was looking for. All over this vast land such communications are repeated thousands of times a day. It is time that all managers adopted the following slogan: *Don't obfuscate—communicate!*

There is yet another kind of communications ability that leaders must have. This ability is not as tangible as writing memos and giving instructions, for this kind of ability requires the manager to be a decent and sympathetic human being. When you are the leader of your organization, your subordinates will be bringing you their personal problems, and whether you want it or not, you'll find yourself fulfilling the role of personal counselor to your people. You'll find yourself listening to all kinds of personal problems that may even be a bit embarrassing. Why? Because as the leader, you have also assumed the role of a father figure—and father is always the one to go to for the resolution of problems. Marital problems, money problems, problems with children—problems of every kind will come your way. How should you react? First of all, become a good listener, but remain a bad advisor. Encourage the people who want to tell you their troubles to seek professional help, but first listen to their troubles without commenting or offering advice; chances are, they are merely looking for a sounding board, for someone to tell their troubles to so that they can get it off their chests for a while. Just by listening you are earning their gratitude and respect. To go further may earn their enmity if the advice is unsound. You will also gain valuable insights into the motivations, personalities, and behavior characteristics of the people in your charge. Understanding them and earning their respect will pay off well for you because of the higher morale that will be generated. You will also be in a position to determine if Joe's or Ethyl's personal problems are so great that they are crippling the effectiveness of the worker in question. Perhaps at this point a problem such as alcoholism could be discussed between you and the employee. If you do get involved in such problems, it would be a very wise idea for you to get some training in human relations or psychology for yourself. Understanding your employees and giving them a sympathetic ear will provide great dividends in loyalty and enthusiasm later on, but don't overdo your role. You're not a father confessor—you're trying to get your organization's business accomplished the best and easiest way possible, and if that means listening to people's troubles for a little while each week, so be it. One caution, however. Respect the confidentiality of those who discuss their personal problems with you. Don't use the information that you have acquired to injure that person.

Finally, there is one other kind of communication process that you will be presiding over. This is the interpersonal communications between co-workers. As manager, you'll have to preside over the relationships within your organization. The compatibility of the people who work for you becomes an extremely important factor in the successful operation of your organization. People who cannot get along with each other shouldn't be placed together. Personal animosities may not seem to be important or may not seem to belong in an organization, but they can play an important role in the efficiency levels that you hope to maintain. Thus, whenever it appears that personality differences are going to affect production, it's up to you, the leader, to do something about it. This requires sensitivity and understanding on your part, but it will be well worth the effort. As Harry Levinson so aptly points out: "When the subordinate is discouraged, confused, and his morale is low, he usually has a hopeless feeling. The tendency of the superior is to reassure him. The superior's quiet trust that the subordinate will surmount his problems is more helpful than reassurance."[3] As a leader, you will be the strong hand, the steady shoulder, the source of confidence and inspiration. That's an important role. Prepare and study for it.

The ability to organize is one of the most important requirements that good executives should have. In a way, the organization of work is as old as the human race. The division and specialization of labor can be traced back to man's prehistoric beginnings. What then is so unique about this ability? The modern era has ushered in new ideas and designs of organizational activity that have been developed with the needs of such technology as mass production and the development of such huge enterprises that they are mind-boggling to contemplate as total entities. Beginning in the era of mass production in the twentieth century then, industrial pioneers such as Henri Fayol or Alfred P. Sloan conceived the ideas that led to organizational theory. They were the first to see the necessity of splitting up an enterprise into subunits or departments, and then integrating the organization by linking the departments in some chain of command. Thus, a huge organization such as General Motors could function more effectively because the subunits would be given the responsibility for *part* of the entire process of production only, while top management would be free to plan and organize the *entire* enterprise. The old hierarchical structures that were envisioned by Fayol and Sloane, however, are thought to be inadequate to today's needs. Today, we hear terms such as "systems management" or "free-form" to describe a new kind of organizational theory based on the belief that the organizational structure should be seen merely as the means of attaining the goals of the organization, nothing else. Therefore, we must first determine what the goals are, and then cut the pattern to fit the cloth. The structure of an organization should never be seen as the end—it is only the means. The following story will illustrate the point.

A new university president had just been appointed. One of his first tasks, as he saw it, was the reorganization of departments and lines of authority. Being new on the job, the president had little acquaintance with the workings of the previous administration. He designed a system that was based on textbook models that had little to do with the realities of the institution. He then had the art department design a flow chart of the lines of authority and the departments that would comprise the new structure of the university. The art department did a magnificent job. The brightly colored boxes and lines were awesome to behold, but within 6 months those beautifully colored charts were as obsolete as the Edsel. I understand they are now prized collectors' items at the same university. Why? Because the new president failed to realize that organizational design comes *last,* not first. You begin with the task, and then design the means for accomplishing that task after you know what it is that you need to accomplish. This means that you must remain flexible, and be ready and willing to tear down old structures as soon as they become obsolete, i.e. as soon as they can no longer serve your purpose.

So the mark of executive ability is to be able to work backward from your goals to the design of a means to attain those goals. The ability to organize is the ability to think through and analyze a systematic approach to solving a problem. Remember, the key to begin with is the problem, *not* the structure.

The ability to plan is closely related to the ability to organize because planning identifies our organizational needs. Without planning there can be no goals, no identification of needs, and no rational pursuit of objectives. Therefore, the successful executive schools himself well in the planning process. What is it that we plan for? Generally speaking, there are three major goals for planning: *Objectives, alternatives,* and *contingencies.*

In planning for objectives, we set down the goals that we hope to achieve, both qualitative and quantitative, and we do this on a long-range as well as on a short-range basis. This does not mean that you now have a sure-fire plan for achievement or a means for avoiding a disaster, but it does mean that you'll have an idea as to where you'll want to be 5, 10, or 20 years from now.

Planning for alternatives is the range of choices that we think are open to us. By exploring alternative choices and other possibilities, we begin to see a whole range of possible developments. While it is true that no one can foretell the future, wisdom dictates that we keep as many alternatives and options as open as possible. One of the common techniques that is used by public relations people is known as "brainstorming." In brainstorming, a group of people commit themselves to meet in a completely democratic, no-holds-barred type of atmosphere. The ground rules during that period are very simple: No idea is too foolish to mention, no animosities are to be carried out of the session, and complete democracy (equality) will be observed during the session. These kinds of exploratory sessions can be extremely successful in discovering new ideas and as an excellent aid in the planning process.

Contingencies are also included as part of the planning process, not because we can plan for every crisis, but because we will at least become nimble-minded enough and aware enough that there are such things as crises, so that we can rise to the occasion when we must. Indeed, contingency planning—planning for crisis—has to be as much a part of the modern world as is normal planning. In the fast-paced world of today, planning has become as much of a necessity as carrying on the function of the organization every day.

The last ability listed was the ability to motivate others. It is also the ability to persuade, not only those who work under your supervision, but those who are above you, and those working alongside you as well. Motivation has been generally described as everything from a kick in the rear to a pat on the head, yet its definition remains very elusive indeed. Part of the problem, of course, is that we tend to measure motivation by results rather than by attitude. Attitude can be generalized; results cannot. The simplest definition I can think of is: *Motivation is getting others to do what you want them to do, and having them think that they had more to do with it than you did.* In other words, motivating others means that you are getting them to operate under their own power. There are more sophisticated psychological theories that explain this process, but perhaps an interesting example will serve our purpose better.

The son of a small manufacturer took over his father's business. The new boss was a nontraditional thinker, and tried the following experiment. He called in each of his employees and asked them to name their own salary. That's right—name your own salary—no matter how ridiculous the figure might seem to you. There were some surprising results from this experiment. First, no employee made any outrageous demands. In most cases, only a few dollars a week more were asked for. Second, the employees began to show more interest in their jobs. One truck driver became much more conscientious, and admitted that he was no longer "goofing off" on the job, as he had been before. What had happened? The employees began to realize that their pay was directly related to production and effort on their part. Further, they were indirectly being asked to make a realistic appraisal of their performances on the job. These realizations made them internalize the goals of the firm and made them understand that their salaries were directly tied to their efforts. This was brought home to them with even greater force than many of the stock-sharing or profit-sharing plans that are now much in vogue. Another experiment was the now famous Volvo experiment in Sweden, where instead of traditional assembly-line practices, a team was assigned to build a complete automobile from start to finish. The responsibility of the team was to set the hours and conditions of work as well as the tasks of each worker. The experiment worked well, but was later abandoned for other reasons. In Yugoslavia, a socialist country, worker-management teams have successfully operated many of that country's basic industries with great success.

According to Frederick Herzberg, writing in The Harvard Business Review's volume *On Management,*[4] people work well or don't work well for the following reasons:

Why they are motivated	*Why they aren't motivated*
Achievement	Company policy and
Recognition	administration
Work itself	Supervision
Responsibility	Relationship with
Advancement	supervisor
Growth	Work conditions
	Salary
	Relationship with peers
	Personal life
	Relationship with
	subordinates
	Status
	Security

The above list is in descending order of importance. Herzberg concludes that what is needed to motivate employees is a promise of self-enrichment that will include widening their areas of responsibility and their possibilities of advancement. Thus, what most people seem to be interested in is the possibility of growth. He who does not grow will begin to shrink. One is tempted to suggest that perhaps that's what life is really all about—growing. Herzberg calls it "vertical enrichment," and that's a good way to remember it. Employees are not particularly motivated by increasing their workloads unless they are given greater responsibility and a greater challenge to their skills. Thus more pay isn't the answer. Achievement and recognition are much more important. Your ability as a manager, therefore, will largely be measured by how well you can give the people under you this sense of achievement and recognition.

Since major United States corporations measure many of their middle level managers periodically, it might be worthwhile considering what the typical large corporation expects from its rising executives. Below is an average listing of the abilities that are expected from a junior executive at a major United States corporation:

People skills
Dedication
Creativity
Ability to communicate verbally
Ability to communicate in writing
Basic business judgment
Initiative
Enthusiasm
Organizational ability
Ability to analyze
Thoroughness
Selection of subordinates
Training of subordinates

These yardsticks of growth are valuable to keep in mind, and they reinforce the kinds of abilities that are most desirable.

Thus, the second rule is: *Study and develop the skills of good management: Decision making, leadership, directing, communicating, organizing, planning, and motivating.*

Beyond the Purple Haze

For many centuries men believed that the sky was blue. Their eyes were not deceiving them. In fact, the sky seemed blue because of the diffusion of light by the earth's atmosphere. Lest we laugh too derisively at our naive ancestors, we should make ourselves aware of the fact that there are many "blue sky" believers in the business and organizational world of today. Such people not only believed the sky was blue; they thought it would remain so forever. Thus, they became victims of their own delusions. For these kinds of people, it is always business as usual, and operating their organizations as though nothing will ever change. Yet, change is the only real constant that we know and will probably ever know.

Recently, a Japanese scientist developed a new transistor that is five times more powerful than the old model. Consider the impact this new development will have on the communications industry, the computer industry, etc. The semiconductor business is one of the fastest growing industries in the world; it has made revolutionary developments in many of the fields that had already been considered permanent. Consider the fact that 40 years ago there were no synthetic fabrics or tires, no nuclear energy, no computers, and little technological development as we understand that term today. Consider further what the next 40 years might bring: All kinds of revolutions in the production and distribution of goods, as well as major scientific and industrial departures. And who knows, perhaps even major changes in social organization. What, then, is the executive to do about all this?

The executive's major task is to be able to see beyond the purple haze that trapped our ancestors into believing that what they saw was all there was to see. The executive of today has to be able to peer around the corner into tomorrow. But does this mean that executives are all about to become no more than gypsy fortune tellers, gazing into fake crystal balls with no more idea of what the future holds than their poor confused customers? No one can know the future. What we must do, therefore, is open our minds and imaginations to the *possibilities*. Even though the realities may be different, it must be considered at least as important to pay attention to future possibilities as to present realities. Opening our minds to the possibilities of the future will require us to develop our skills in three major areas: Innovation, creativity, and awareness.

Today's successful manager is an innovator first, and a production man second. He must be highly flexible, adjust easily to new conditions, and develop new techniques constantly. Major industries and corporations have increased their research activity more than eightfold within the past 30 years. Much of their research has been not only in new product development, but in the development of new techniques as well. The constant search for newer and easier methods of running organizations is never ending. In fact, it has been considerably speeded up by the nature of international competition. The lesson is clear: *Innovation is the key to survival.*

Creativity is also one of those skills that is perhaps not present in all of us. If not, the successful manager will do his best to encourage creativity among his subordinates. Creativity means thinking out new processes, imagining the unimaginable, and trying out the unthinkable. In the past few years, for example, a host of new ideas has resulted in enormously expanded business possibilities in specialty items. A gentleman by the name of Amos marketed a chocolate chip cookie ("Famous Amos") that became a nationwide success. Men's blue jeans used to be sold to women, but they were ill-fitting. Today's creative apparel designers are coming out with lines of blue jeans more suited to the female silhouette. New businesses have even been developed from singing telegrams to dog walking. All of these were the products of someone's creative urge—someone who thought "why not?" No one would ever have thought that you could sell rocks to people. But one young man thought up the idea of Pet Rocks and did a landslide business of selling the "Pet Rock" to people all over the country one Christmas season. The little rocks were attractively packaged, and came with witty instructions for their care. The above are examples of creating a new business from scratch, and you may say, "That's fine for them, but I'm part of a huge organization. How does all that apply to me?" On a larger scale, the same kind of creativity is being called for every day. New possibilities, products, ideas, and developments are being called for in the desperate battle for survival. Even as you are reading this now, thousands of new inventions and ideas that could change our daily lives are being contemplated and developed. Your role as a rising star is either to develop your creativity or to appreciate and develop the creative skills in those who work for you or with you.

The Hudson's Bay Company is the world's oldest mercantile organization. It has been in business for 309 years, ever since it was first chartered in 1670 by King Charles in England. What has been their secret of survival in an age when large corporate giants have had to be placed on the auctioneers' blocks? The Hudson's Bay people originally meant it to be a fur trading organization, but realized it had to change and adjust with the times. It met this challenge to its innovative powers by establishing one of the most far-flung retail operations in the entire world. In Canada, the world's second largest country geographically, the Hudson's Bay Company operates over 300 outlets from downtown Toronto to Baffin Island, far into the frozen arctic. They no longer trade in furs, but they do trade in just about everything else you could think of. The Hudson's Bay Company provides a good lesson for all of us in the advantage of remaining aware and innovative. They may have had early advantages in the form of a royal monopoly from King Charles, but they could easily have gone as bankrupt as anyone else in Canada if they hadn't made good use of their wits as well as their wills to survive.

Awareness of new ideas, new developments, and new information is certainly part of every successful executive's baggage. Many corporations today give their executives sabbatical leaves simply because they realize that an executive who is well-informed about the world around him is a much more astute and valuable person to have in the organization. Awareness is information, and that is where the crunch of the future will come. Management specialists tell us that the role of managers is changing rapidly. No longer are they going to be concerned with production—their role will lie in making future projections over the next 10 or 20 years. Their chief ally will be information. The collecting, storing, and digesting of such information will surely become the most important responsibility that managers of the future will have. Even in the animal world only the collection of information can assure survival. Honey bees, for example, constantly scout new locations for colonies to be established. The scouts find suitable locations for the new colonies, and then, in a kind of dance, tell the queen about their discoveries. She then makes the decision for the establishment of new colonies, based on her scouts' intelligence. Awareness! If bees can collect and store information as their chief key to survival, shouldn't we sit up and take notice? There's an old saying, "The more we know, the more we realize how little we know." Your role as a manager will not be measured so much as by how well you can prod others; instead, it will be measured by how much information you have and how aware you are, because you must be as much in touch with the future as the present. Only in this way, will you ever penetrate the purple haze.

Our third rule, then, is: *Penetrate the purple haze. Acquire the skills of innovation, creativity, and awareness.*

DISCOVER YOUR ABILITY

Self-appraisal is one of the most difficult arts there is because we really cannot stand back and take a long, objective look at ourselves. Therefore, we must rely on others to help us. If we accept the fact that no one is perfect and that a little constructive criticism is a good idea, then we must be willing to solicit criticisms of our performance from three sources: Our superiors, our subordinates, and our peers.

All too frequently, appraisals of our work are buried in the minds of those around us, and only grudgingly revealed (usually in some kind of explosion during an argument). It makes much more sense, therefore, to ask for a periodic review of weaknesses as well as strengths, and if it is not company policy, make it one of your tasks to ask your superiors, "How am I doing?", "What are my weak areas?", "How would you suggest that I improve?" Such requests are bound to create a favorable impression, and what's more important, will give you the appraisal that you need.

Similarly, asking those who work for you to appraise your abilities is not a sign of weakness; it's a sign of intelligence, and if properly designed, will clear the air of suspicions and alienation. Most important, however, is the benefit of knowing how well you are being received, and how those who work for you see you. That will be your best mirror. Sometimes, it takes a lot of courage to look into a clear mirror. Our warts as well as our more comely features are all there, however, and we must take a long hard look at our virtues as well as our weaknesses if we are to succeed. There can be no intelligent self-appraisal without the help of others.

Our fourth rule, then, is: *Seek the appraisal of your abilities from your superiors, your subordinates, and your peers.*

SUMMARY

Executives are among the most mobile of Americans. They move from job to job, especially in their early years, and this will create opportunity for rising young managers like you. Some of the major reasons that executives fail are: inflexibility, poor delegation of authority, poor time management, poor communications, and poor morale. There are several kinds of abilities that make effective managers, and these can all be acquired. They are: the abilities to lead, decide, direct, communicate, organize, plan, and motivate.

The reasons that some organizations are successful, and others are not, are that successful management has the ability to innovate; that it is creative; and that it is aware of the impending developments of the future. Future sensitivity can only be developed by education and awareness. Finally, the responsibility for self-improvement is directly tied to an accurate appraisal of your strengths as well as your weaknesses; you should try to obtain appraisals from three sources: your superiors, your subordinates, and your peers.

THE FOUR RULES FOR DEVELOPING ABILITY

1. Learn the pitfalls that lead to executive failure, and how to avoid them: Inflexibility, poor delegation of authority, poor time management, poor communications, and poor motivation.
2. Develop the basic skills of good management: Decision making, leadership, directing, communicating, organizing, planning, and motivating others.
3. Be able to penetrate the purple haze. Innovation, creativity, and awareness must be developed.
4. Have yourself appraised by your superiors, your subordinates, and your peers. Do not be afraid to look in the mirror!

EXERCISES FOR CHAPTER 3

1. Brainstorming

Try a brainstorming session. Use the rules of the brainstorming game as outlined in this chapter. The session should last no longer than 1 hour and should deal with the solution of some problem. Get a group of three or four people together. Any manageably sized group is alright. Most importantly, the group should be quite familiar with the problem to be solved.

2. Self-appraisal

Develop a questionnaire that can be answered by your subordinates; do it in such a way that they can answer anonymously and without fear of reprisal. Your questionnaire can be simple, yet highly instructive for your progress. Here is one sample:

Questionnaire

Please answer the following by placing a check in the most appropriate answer box, using a scale of 1 to 5, with 1 being the lowest or poorest mark you would give, and 5 being the best or highest mark you would give.

	1	2	3	4	5
1. Does your boss give you clear easily understood directions?					
2. Do you find your boss easy to talk to, or are you afraid to speak up to him/her?					
3. Do you think that your boss is a leader who inspires you to do your job better?					
4. Do you feel enthusiastic about your job?					

Try to develop your own questionnaire. Just making up the questions that you would ask will provide valuable insights for you.

3. Beyond the purple haze

Research the future. Go to your local library and read magazines that deal with contemporary developments that will profoundly affect our future. Two good examples of such magazines are "Scientific American" and "The World Future Society's Journal." Save newspaper clippings or trade magazine articles that deal with events that are happening now that will affect your future.

NOTES

1. Ralph Waldo Emerson, *Essays*. A. L. Burt and Company, New York (no date). p. 229.

2. Cameron Hawley, *Executive Suite.* Houghton Mifflin, Boston, 1952. pp. 330–334.

3. Harry Levinson, *The Exceptional Executive.* Mentor Books, New American Library, New York, 1971. p. 203.

4. Frederick Herzberg, "One more time: How do you motivate employees?," in *On Management* (Harvard Business Review), Harper and Row, New York, 1975. pp. 361 ff.

4

Nonconformity

Don't Be a Clone

Twenty-five years ago "the man in the gray flannel suit" or "the organization man" were the perfect stereotypes of the rising young executive. Today, such stereotypes are no longer valid. Corporations have found that they cannot cope with a world of lightning-fast changes and daily challenges to their hopes for survival, by having a bunch of "yes men"—robots in gray flannel suits—managing their affairs. The day of the corporate clone is indeed over, and the nonconformist, the individualist, and the creative thinker are rapidly taking center stage.

There is an inherent conflict in the need for presenting a unified front to the world for the organization that you work for, and in stimulating the kind of original thinking that can come only from dissent. There is also a kind of basic conflict between the goals of the organization, sometimes known as the "corporate image," and the beliefs or values of the individual who is asked to play a role in guiding that organization's future. If you are asked to be a leader, you are being asked because of your brains, not because of your beauty. The organization that you work for can go out and hire 10 or 20 models or movie stars to enhance their public image on television or whatever medium may be in vogue. But only *you* have the unique qualities that will avert disaster and bring success. An interesting example comes to mind. In 1978, the Firestone Tire and Rubber Company, faced with a number of consumer complaints and a number of serious accidents on the highway that were alleged to have been the result of faulty radial tires, finally agreed to a recall of their product. This, of course, has resulted in a major financial loss to the company. Firestone then went out and hired the famed movie star, Jimmy Stewart, to repair its public image by doing a series of television commercials at a price that was reported in the press to be around $1,000,000. All that money, time, and aggravation could have been saved if there had been more honest dissent within the organization, and if the top management had been courageous enough to face the fact that there was something to the complaints of the public. It is ironic also to consider that Jimmy Stewart's pitch was to characterize Harvey Firestone as an original thinker and creative dissenter, who would be satisfied with nothing but the best. If Harvey Firestone was an executive at the corporation that bears his name today, he probably would have had very tough sledding trying to convince the company that it should change its product instead of its pitch.

Nonconformity, dissent, creative conflict, or whatever handle you wish to use are obviously valuable tools, but like all tools, they have to be used carefully and with thoughtful consideration. Let's look at some of the pitfalls that face the individualist, and some of the reasons that he is more valuable to the corporation or organization than a thousand corporate clones.

First, we must remind ourselves that ever since group efforts became the primary method for most human endeavors, there has always been the need to protect the group, even if it must be at the expense of the individual.

Hence, the outsider who might destroy or threaten the group is seen as a villain. Similarly, anyone who threatens the cohesion of the group is likely to be branded as a destructive individual. This dilemma has been at the root of the conflict between individualism and the needs of the group (or organization) since civilization began. Thus, all organizations tend to regard dissenters as oddballs, freaks, or worse. The challenge to the creative person who sees the need for change is to present that need in such a way that it will not be perceived as a threat to the organization's existence. Obviously, that's not an easy thing to do.

Second, although conflict is never very pleasant, it has to be seen as an energizer. That is, it is a process that creates the energy that your organization will feed on. Conflict also means disorder to a lot of people. To many executives, it represents something untidy; loose ends; things undone or coming undone. For others, it represents failure and inadequacy ("Now, why couldn't *I* have thought of that?" moans the frustrated manager to himself).

Third, those who are rocking the boat can easily become feared and distrusted by the others who are manning the oars. Change represents insecurity to most, adventure to only a few; and those who advocate change are apt to suffer the arrows and slings of scorn, rather than the praise they might expect. The Chinese people are renowned for their inventiveness as well as for their diligence. But what is not well known is that in ancient Chinese society, inventors of labor-saving devices were sometimes put to death because their inventions put people out of work! But this is the twentieth century, and the demand for innovation is greater than ever, even in China.

Nonconformity has many more positive aspects than negative ones. For one thing, it gives birth to the tensions that will later release their creative forces within the organization. The tensions between those who want to try something new or do something different are bound to clash with those who want the old order just as it has been. Such tension is bound to result in the release of tremendous amounts of creative energy which will ultimately benefit the organization in a welter of new ideas. Nonconformity also allows management to see the other side of an issue. If no one were to play devil's advocate, there never would be much objectivity when it comes to decision making. Thus, decision making would not be a rational process, but an irrational one, based on the prejudice (and pride) of one man or a few men with like minds. This could become a very dangerous process. As Henry Ford grew older and more set in his ways, he refused to agree to new marketing methods for his automobiles. The company faced ruin because design and marketing were all controlled by a group of highly inbred cronies that Ford had gathered around him. This bunch of "yes men" did not allow the light of controversy to filter into the company, hence when General Motors came onto the market with new ideas and product innovations, the Ford Motor Company's monopoly of the automobile market began to slip badly. Ford's fortunes were finally saved only when Henry Ford II took over the management of the company and hired a group of managers, some of them from General Motors, to contribute their "nonconformity" to Ford's salvation. Among the new group of managers was Robert S. McNamara, who later became Secretary of Defense under President John F. Kennedy. Incidentally, McNamara was hired by Kennedy, even though he was a Republican, because of the highly innovative methods that he had developed at Ford as well as when he was a professor at Harvard Business School. By all accounts, McNamara was the most startling event of the postwar period at the Department of Defense because of the new methods and insights that he provided. No one had ever rocked the boat as much as McNamara did, and his tenure paid off handsomely in a more efficiently organized agency.

Nonconformists provide new insights and new perspectives for their organizations, and the result usually is the ability to consider the impossible. The legendary generals who were considered to be strategic geniuses (such as MacArthur, Rommel, Grant, Washington, Montgomery, etc.) were all successful because they considered the impossible—they put themselves in the enemy's shoes, and then asked, "Why not?" You simply cannot put yourself in your adversary's place unless you are willing (and able) to engage in nonconformist thinking. So to succeed, we must get out of that rut and start down the road toward the impossible, the unconsidered, the unattainable, the inconceivable, and the imponderable—they're not so impossible after all!

Our first rule, then, is: *Don't become a clone. Realize that nonconformity is at the root of all great endeavors.*

IT'S THEIR STYLE THAT BEGUILES

Individualism and nonconformity are on the opposite sides of the same coin. They are supplementary to each other, and certainly, one cannot exist without the other. What marks off one individual from another is his/her style. "The style makes the man," goes an old adage, but it is as true today as it was 100 years ago. As managers, each of us will approach any given problem in a different way. We will pursue the solution of that problem in a slightly different way, with different perceptions, and probably with different results. Our styles can get us into a great deal of trouble; they can also be our salvation, depending on how we use them. One thing is clear, however—without style, without your individualism, you are "as naked as a jaybird." With style you are clothed with the uniqueness of your personality, your perceptions, your intelligence, and all that makes you tick as a human being. Value your individualism and your style; they make you special. Individualism, style, nonconformity—none of them knows a special age or special condition. It would be instructive for us to take a look at a few good examples of people who were nonconformists and made their nonconformity pay off because they knew what they wanted and had a plan for achieving their goals.

Frederick Tudor

"A slippery prospect," scoffed one Boston newspaper when it learned of Frederick Tudor's plan to ship ice to the tropics in 1803. Many agreed that it was a ridiculous idea, but Tudor had an obsession that would not leave him alone. He was also an individualist who refused to go to Harvard College. "It was for loafers," he later said, and he opted instead to strike out on his own, even though his father was a prosperous Boston merchant. When he died in 1864 at the age of 81, Tudor was worth well over $1,-000,000, and had salvaged his family's fortune as well (his well-to-do father had gone bankrupt).

So famous did his scheme become, and so tightly was he able to establish a monopoly over the ice trade, that Tudor became known as "the Ice King" and always reveled in that nickname. His idea of shipping ice had to be refined and worked out; and in order to develop markets, he had to create a demand for his product. Ice had to be harvested from the lakes and ponds of New England, and then shipped in airtight cargo holds, insulated with sawdust from sawmills in Maine. All of these ideas had to be developed from scratch, but Tudor was unrelenting and never lost sight of his goals. His first attempt to develop a market was in the tropical West Indies, in Martinique, where he landed a cargo of ice in July, 1803. No one knew what to do with the ice. Few had ever seen any ice before, and the ice was quickly melting on the docks. Finally, Tudor was able to convince the proprietor of a local coffee house that ice cream would go over well. The proprietor agreed, and Tudor started manufacturing ice cream right then and there. When the sweltering customers began gobbling up the new delight, Tudor knew he had found a market, and the doubting proprietor, seeing the success of the new product, became in Tudor's words, " ... as humble as a mushroom." Tudor went on to greater exploits with his ice trade and became the first exporter to land a cargo of 150 tons of ice successfully in India—a 5-month voyage around

Cape Horn—with less than 10 percent of it having melted. He built ice houses in New Orleans, Charleston, India, and the West Indies that could keep the ice from melting despite the tropical heat. What was Tudor's secret of success? He didn't see the obstacles—he just saw the goals.

A. Ernest Fitzgerald

A. Ernest Fitzgerald will probably go down in history as "the man who blew the whistle." He rose to a comfortable $31,000-a-year job as a top-ranking federal bureaucrat in the Air Force by 1969. That year, his testimony before a committee of Congress uncovered a major scandal. The controversial C-5A aircraft transport, he said, had cost billions more due to cost overruns that were the product of incompetency on the part of administration officials. This started a round of investigation that was to last more than a year, and resulted in a great deal of embarrassment for the Nixon administration. Shortly after Mr. Fitzgerald's testimony before Congress, during which he pointed out that cost overruns and other fixing schemes were common practice by administration officials who were conniving with defense industry contractors to drive prices higher, H. R. Haldeman, Chief of the White House staff, got a memo from Alexander Butterfield, deputy assistant to President Nixon, that Fitzgerald's lack of loyalty should be punished. "After all," said Butterfield, "loyalty is the name of the game." Apparently, Fitzgerald didn't think so. At any rate, he was summarily dismissed from his job.

Fitzgerald then appealed his dismissal to the Civil Service Commission, but he got nowhere. Then began the nightmare of legal appeals and litigation with expensive lawyers that was to cost him almost $400,000, a sum of money that he didn't have. After 4 years, Fitzgerald won his appeal at the Civil Service Commission and was reinstated in a similar job, at a slightly higher salary than his old one. So justice had been done, but at terrible expense, and Fitzgerald's reward for blowing the whistle on greedy contractors was a huge legal bill that he was unable to pay. Fitzgerald then did something that was unprecedented. He sued the Civil Service Commission for his legal fees, and won! A federal district judge agreed that the government had a responsibility to those who have been wrongfully dismissed from their jobs. Mr. Fitzgerald today is an Undersecretary of the United States Air Force. He still feels that he has suffered greatly for his courage and nonconformity, but wouldn't do anything differently because it's not his style. As a result of the courage displayed by Fitzgerald and a few other federal executives, President Jimmy Carter and the United States Congress made an outstanding provision in the Civil Service Reform Act. Title I of that act is called "whistleblower protection," and prohibits reprisals against an employee who discloses to the public or to other federal officials a violation of a law, rule, or regulation; mismanagement; waste of funds; abuse of authority or substantial and specific danger to public health and safety.

Were it not for the courage and tenacity of federal executives like A. Ernest Fitzgerald, such a law would probably never have gotten on the books. Fitzgerald got no huge rewards and didn't make any fortunes, but he derived a great deal of satisfaction; and that was what really counted for him. Fitzgerald had to live with his conscience and could not take the easy road that other bureaucrats had by lying to Congress. His own sense of integrity led him to take a nonconformist position.

Henry J. Kaiser

"Problems are opportunities in work clothes," was a favorite saying of the man who was undoubtedly the most flamboyant and inventive industrialist of the twentieth century. Born of German immigrant parents in 1882, he left school at an early age and went to work for a dry goods firm. He began taking photographs in his spare time, and finally went into the photography business full time in upstate New York. In 1903, he was promised a partnership in a successful photography establishment, if he could double its volume. Henry tripled the volume, and was made a partner. Three years later, after successfully opening many new branches, Henry Kaiser gave it all up and headed for Spokane, Washington, where he went to work for a hardware store owner with a surplus stock of silverware. Henry quickly got rid of the silverware, turned over a handsome profit for the firm, and was made sales manager. Henry Kaiser had already begun to demonstrate that the more normal route of slow advancement with one firm was not going to be his cup of tea.

In 1909, Henry Kaiser went to work for a gravel and cement firm, the Hawkeye Company of Spokane, where he learned the business, and then, in 1914, he founded his first corporation, the Henry J. Kaiser Company, of Vancouver. Henry Kaiser once again began to demonstrate his flair for the unusual and unconventional, and won huge paving contracts by underbidding larger firms and by beating his competition to the punch. It was not long before Kaiser had become one of the largest road builders on the West Coast. He was constantly innovating and always looking for newer and cheaper methods of getting a job done. When other contractors were still using horse teams to build roads, he was using tractors. He could build roads in less than half the time of his competitors. Kaiser's first big break was a construction contract for 200 miles of roads in Cuba. He finished it in less than half the stipulated time, and together with his son, Edgar, went on to become one of the principals in the construction of the world's largest and most complex projects up to that time, the Hoover Dam. It was a great challenge for the ingenuity of Kaiser Construction, for new methods had to be developed to tackle a job that had no known precedents. The Hoover Dam was completed in 5 years instead of 7, no small thanks to Henry J. Kaiser and his "whiz kids." From there, Kaiser Construction went on to build the Bonneville Dam in 1938 and The Grand Coulee Dam in 1940. Other giant construction projects followed, but it was shipbuilding that beckoned Kaiser.

In 1942, Henry J. Kaiser began a shipbuilding business, the likes of which had never been seen before. He began construction of the famous liberty ships; as production peaked, they were sliding down the ways at the rate of one every 4 days. He was the first to develop the prefabricated method of construction, and one of his shipyards set a world's record of having completely built a liberty ship in 4 days, 15 hours, and 26 minutes. By the time that World War II was over, Henry J. Kaiser's shipbuilding firms had built almost 1,500 ships, including 50 small aircraft carriers. Indeed, it could be said that Kaiser's creativity meant the difference between death and survival for England, when the convoys had to be replenished in the war with the German U-boats.

After World War II, Kaiser decided to enter the automobile business, and teamed up with Joe Frazer to produce the Kaiser-Frazer automobiles. Again with his flamboyance and flair for the new and unusual, Kaiser-Frazer came out with cars whose styling and engineering were advanced far beyond their time. Frontwheel drive, fiberglass bodies, and aerodynamic styling were among the major innovations. He was also among the first to introduce a compact car—The Henry J—to the market. Kaiser's foray into the automobile business failed by 1952, not because of any lack of creativity, but because of underfinancing and shortages of materials. Even in this business he ran the world's longest assembly line, Willow Run, which he purchased for production of the Kaiser-Frazer automobiles.

Kaiser never thought of himself as a miracle man, just a man who enjoyed meeting new challenges and building organizations composed of people he could depend on. Henry Kaiser's real secret, however, was the zest that he always had for these new challenges. He approached them as though they were some kind of a new game to be mastered, and then went on to the next one. That was probably his secret, and thus is a lesson for us. Enthusiasm for new challenges and new opportunities is one of the things that lies at the core of creative leadership.

Julius Rosenwald and Robert E. Wood

Sears, Roebuck, and Company is the world's largest retailer. With sales in excess of $10 billion annually, Sears sells just about everything that the American consumer could think of. Few people today would stop to think about it, but Sears, Roebuck is the product of the innovative genius of two men, Julius Rosenwald (1862–1932) and Robert E. Wood (1879–1969). When Rosenwald took over Sears, Roebuck at the turn of the century, it was a bankrupt mail order house for distressed merchandise. Rosenwald saw something else that no one in his day had yet really thought about. More than 50 percent of the population of the United States still lived in rural areas, and they were rapidly acquiring more needs for manufactured goods than the nation's antiquated distribution system could supply them with. Rosenwald, with keen intuition, sensed this need, and quickly turned the Sears, Roebuck operation into a huge mail order house that could supply the American farmer and his family with quality merchandise sold with the unprecedented guarantee, "Satisfaction guaranteed or your money back." No other merchandising operation had been willing to make such an offer to the American consumer, and Sears rapidly developed into the nation's largest mail order house. Rosenwald, in order to handle the huge volume of orders and produce satisfactory merchandise, delivered on time, had to develop reliable sources of supply, and a system for the mass handling of mail orders. To do this, he contracted with suppliers over a long term, and in many cases invested in the manufacturers as well. His mass production lines for the assembly of mail orders was a marvel of the times. It was said that this innovation influenced Henry Ford's development of his automobile assembly lines. Thus, Sears, Roebuck became the nation's first mass supplier of consumer goods, and the Sears catalogue became as familiar as the family Bible.

Rosenwald hired Robert Wood because he was impressed with his performance as an executive at Montgomery Ward, where he began to predict the demise of the farmer as a market for the mail order business. Wood was right, and he used his knowledge of trends and projections to help reshape Sears, Roebuck. Under Wood's guiding innovative genius, Sears began to aim for the urban middle class market by building a chain of retail stores from coast to coast, and by stocking those stores with the goods that the new American middle classes were beginning to be able to purchase, such as refrigerators, stoves, washing machines, and sewing machines. Sears went into the mass manufacturing markets as well to get the kinds of goods that could sell cheaply and be maintained by Sears servicemen. It was this second great expansion Wood undertook that made Sears the world's largest retailer that it is today. Wood also guided Sears into selling insurance, servicing and selling automobile parts, and finally, designing shopping centers that were the beginnings of surburban America. Sears, Roebuck thus became the product of men who were not afraid to be innovative, and were unwilling to remain conformist in their thinking. Instead they tried to move ahead of the trends, and predict the future shape of consumerism in America. In a competitive world, successful management is more a product of innovative creativity than pedestrian storekeeping.

Alexander Dingee

Alexander Dingee is an innovator who searches for other innovators. He founded, 10 years ago, an enterprise which has become unique. Venture Founders, Inc. is an organization that searches for and trains people to be entrepreneurs in areas that are economically depressed or underdeveloped. Dingee has made a study of the problem, and pointed out, "Our basic premise is that the major factor in the success of a venture is the entrepreneur and the team around him—and that's what most venture capitalists and bankers say."

Dingee's firm has contracted with foreign governments and with communities in the more depressed areas of the

United States to find and develop good business talent rather than losing promising young talented people to other parts of the country. Dingee's formula for the successful entrepreneur sounds very much like the same one for a successful innovator: good reaction to failure ("I'll try again. I won't give up."), tenacity, the ability to set goals, the ability to take risks, good verbal ability, and the ability to be realistic.

At the present time, Dingee's firm has been operating very successfully in Nova Scotia, one of Canada's most depressed provinces. Those who successfully qualify as entrepreneurs are then given priority for government subsidized loans for going into business for themselves, and many have proven to be highly successful.

There are probably thousands more like the above examples of people who refuse to be slaves to conformity. Each of the persons cited above had a highly individualized approach to problem-solving. Yet, with each there is a discernably different method of tackling the problems confronted. It is the methodology and the approach that we can learn from and put to use in our own behalf. How can we categorize, and how can we best learn to apply this principle of nonconformity, or style, to ourselves? Or put another way, how can we learn what style of managerial behavior we should follow? How can we know what is the "correct" style for us to use, and can we adapt ourselves to any style of leadership? We may admire nonconformist behavior, dashing courage, authoritarian style, and many other different kinds of style that have been adapted by executives, many of whom we are in daily contact with. To what extent we should model ourselves and our behavior after those we see in positions of leadership is an interesting question. There are obvious limits on our behavior and on our individuality. We cannot lead our lives exactly as we want to—a degree of conformity to the standards of society and to the organization that we work for is certainly requisite. But within that narrow framework of conformity, there is room, plenty of room really, for the individual to develop his own style—one that will be comfortable for him, consonant with his beliefs, and yet still mark him off as an individual who thinks for himself. There are four major factors that determine what kind of style you will have for yourself. These are: personality, character, values, and environment. Let's take a look at each one, and try to determine how you can best go about building a style that is good for you and that can best represent you. It is important that you give this careful attention because chances are you have never realized how very important it is for an aspiring leader like yourself to begin establishing your "M.O." *(modus operandi).*

Personality

A very interesting study that attempts to analyze the personality types that executives fall into was recently published by Michael Maccoby[1]. In it, Maccoby carefully described four personality types that can identify most leaders. These are: the craftsman, the jungle fighter, the company man, and the gamesman. The craftsman is a person who enjoys building. He is interested in doing a professional job and being able to stand back and admire his handiwork. He is very much of the persuasion that the Protestant ethic with its values on work, thrift, quality, production, and process is still the best way to go. He wants *good* workmanship no matter what the task. The craftsman is much more comfortable in a structured environment than in an unstructured one. He does not want to create new systems or be placed in informal or highly complex organizations with highly involved relationships. Instead, the craftsman is highly dependent on his organization because it gives him orientation and direction for his work, hence, a feeling of security. The craftsman is not particularly interested in manipulating others, and prefers to be led rather than do the leading. A good example of a craftsman type who is in a position of authority might be the head research engineer or the head research chemist of a large organization. Their positions are authoritative and creative, but only in the more narrowly confined structure of the organization that they work for.

The jungle fighter is a personality type who plays for keeps. To his way of thinking, survival is a serious problem, and he always sees himself threatened by the other predators in the forest. There are two kinds of jungle fighters—lions and foxes. Lions are those who conquer by aggression and who seek to command all that they conquer with unquestioned authority. For the lions, there can be no rivals. Foxes are those who are also anxious to conquer, but they prefer to do so by stealth and manipulation. While the lion wants to conquer and carve out new territories (empires) for himself, the fox is the kind of person who wants to rise through the hierarchy to the top. The jungle fighter, whether he is a lion or a fox, feels threatened most of the time because he sees himself constantly at war for territorial gain, for money, etc. The law of the jungle—destroy or be destroyed—dominates this type of individual.

The company man is one who believes strongly in teamwork. He is very similar to the organization man that was discussed earlier in this chapter. For him, the company is the beginning and the end of all that he strives for. Without the company, in fact, he finds little purpose in life and is unable to function well as a lonely thinker or as a solitary worker. The company man needs the stimulation and support of the other members of the organization, and probably finds a great sense of security in being able to relate to this organization and its members in a humanistic way. In many ways, the company man is a highly sociable fellow and can relate to other people quite well.

The gamesman is a child of the 1960s and 1970s when we became faced with new and unusual problems related to consumerism, government regulation, energy shortages, inflation, international problems, etc. This new era required a great deal of intuitive thinking and creativity, and the gamesman was just the person for it. The gamesman enjoys his position only if it is challenging, and only if he can make a game out of it so that he can have the ultimate pleasure—winning. As the late Vince Lombardi used to say, "Winning isn't everything—it's the *only* thing." Being able to snatch the brass ring is the challenge that the gamesman enjoys. Thus, he is somewhat different from the jungle fighter who wants power for power's sake. The gamesman would only enjoy his power if he could use it in some creative way. Otherwise, he would probably become easily bored just being king of the forest. Gamesmen are constantly having their ingenuity tested, and part of the challenge that any gamesman faces will be the survival of his company. Gamesmen that have no new challenges to face can become very unhappy people. Placing them in highly structured situations or giving them humdrum jobs can be a death sentence and could lead to self destructive practices such as alcoholism. Moreover, it would be a great tragedy to any organization not to fully utilize the energy and spirit of the gamesman.

Of course, none of the above four types are absolute stereotypes of individuals. We are all composite personalities. It is simply that in most of us there are these dominant strains of personality types that seem to point us down a particular road, and probably go a long way in explaining why certain kinds of people occupy the positions that they do.

There is one other personality type important to consider. This one is described by Robert N. McMurry in *The Maverick Executive.*[2] According to McMurry's study, the maverick executive is cut from different cloth. He is a workaholic filled with boundless energy; he takes pride in making his own decisions; he seeks to rule by influencing others rather than by dominating them; he is not an anxious type; he relies more heavily on hunches and intuition than empirical evidence; he is not patient; he believes in the work ethic, and holds strongly to his values; he does not believe in team management; he is not a permissive boss, and demands a great deal from his subordinates; finally, he is not an idealist, but a pragmatist. The maverick can be frequently unappreciated by his organization, but his nontraditional approach to problems can make him a very valuable asset. Undoubtedly, he would be regarded as a heavy cross to bear by many co-workers.

As a nonconformist and as a dissenter, the maverick executive can perform a great service to his organization. He can point out flaws that others either cannot see or are afraid to mention; he can play the devil's advocate, which is both an undesirable but a highly necessary role for someone in the organization to play; finally, by his own pigheadedness, he can frequently persevere to overcome obstacles that would have defeated anyone else long ago.

Table 4-1 outlines some of the characteristics of the personality types that were described.

You should be able to utilize this chart to type your own personality and discover where you belong. In the exercise section, follow the suggested exercise.

Character

A second determinant of what kind of style you'll develop for yourself is what is known as character (attitude). James D. Barber in his study, *Presidential Character,*[3] has

Table 4–1
Characteristics of Personality Types Described.

	Likes to work with others	More interested in product than in process	Likes to manip- ulate others	Wants to command	Would rather feel secure	Always enjoys a challenge
Craftsman	Yes	Yes	No	Perhaps	Yes	No
Jungle fighter	Yes	No	Yes	Yes	No	No
Company man	Yes	No	No	No	Yes	No
Games man	Yes	No	Yes	Yes	No	Yes
Maverick	No	No	Yes	Yes	No	Yes

given valuable insights into executive character, and even though his study applies only to American presidents, Barber has made some shrewd analyses of the different kinds of attitudes that executives, whether they are of the political variety or the corporate variety, bring with them to their jobs.

Barber defines four types of presidential character, drawing upon history and biographical portraits of the men he studied. The four types are:

Active-positive. This type of individual has a positive attitude toward his work, the world, and his goals. He believes in himself, and he believes that he will be able to accomplish whatever it is that he sets out to do. He sees himself as being able to fulfill his potential and growing considerably in the process. Moreover, this type of personality enjoys his work and is a highly active person as well. He believes in applying himself as completely as possible to the goals that he has announced for himself with drive and energy.

Active-negative. This type of individual is an extremely hard worker who puts great effort into whatever he wants to do. The main difference between this type and the previous type is that the active-negative person feels that even though he works hard and puts forth much effort, all his hard work will be ultimately unsuccessful. He has a poor self-image as a successful executive, even though he may be very successful in fact, and he is constantly in fear of his environment which he judges to be hostile and unfriendly. Such a person does not really believe that his efforts, heroic as they might be, will ever really be very fruitful.

Passive-positive. This kind of character has low self-esteem, is not particularly aggressive toward the external world, and instead seeks approval and encouragement. Yet, the passive-positive type is an optimist, and believes that he will be able to accomplish his goals. The passive-positive type believes that he will somehow muddle through and achieve success after all, because others will help him to succeed or because events will turn his way.

The passive-positive type depends heavily on others for his success, and can therefore also be labeled a company man as well.

Passive-negative. A generally pessimistic attitude combined with a feeling of low self-esteem characterizes this type. There is an air of hopelessness that generates a great deal of dependence on others for the fulfillment of goals. This type tends also to be inflexible and somewhat rigid in his views. Passive-negative types tend to escape into systems and complex organizations that can provide a safe niche for them, rather than trying to face problems boldly. They depend heavily on others for approval as well as for accomplishment.

The above analysis of character shows that the most desirable character for an executive to have is the first type, the active-positive; while the least desirable is the last type, the passive-negative. Nevertheless, all types can be found in command of an organization, even of a country, because these types, as we suggested before, identify men who were presidents of the United States at one time or another. The significance of these studies of executive personality makes them important for your consideration because they will serve as a guide for yourself, and also will help to identify the characters of those in your organization who can help you or hurt you in your rise to the top. For example, you may be associated with an executive who is of the craftsman type and who has an active-negative character. This kind of person will require good, thorough workmanship from you, and will expect lots of effort. He also will need great support from you as well, as this type needs a great deal of external moral support. For such support as you can give this kind of person, you will undoubtedly be greatly rewarded. You should also spend some time and energy discovering your own character, so that you can find the kind of environment that will be comfortable for you, and so that you can work in a setting that will be complementary, not hostile and unsuitable. This brings us to our second rule: *Study the different character and personality types. Learn to analyze yourself as*

*well as the people around you. Above all, learn to accom-
modate yourself by becoming complementary to those on
whom your advancement depends.*

Values

Values make up the third major component of your
style. Although values are intangible assets, they are the
core of your soul, and they are those beliefs, inherited or
acquired, that make you different from anyone else. Values also form the basis of your belief system, and most of
your behavior can be traced to your values. That is, you
will orient your activity, and behave only in a way that is
consonant with your values. Acting in a manner that is not
in harmony with your system of values is bound to produce deep conflict within you, and sooner or later will
result in much unhappiness and dissatisfaction with yourself. Therefore, understanding the values that you prize
most is a key to your own behavior and will certainly help
to guide you to a position and an organization that will be
supportive of your values. Suppose you work in an environment with values that do not agree with yours. Chances
are you will be unable to adjust your values to the environment, and sooner or later, you'll have to come to grips with
the fact that your values simply do not agree with those of
your organization, your boss, your administration, or
whatever. At that point, you must realize what the differences are, and if it appears that you cannot rationalize
these differences, you would probably be well advised to
change your environment, for you cannot change your basic beliefs. Therefore, it becomes important for you to clar-
ify your values, and to discover for yourself the kind of
person that you are, what you believe in, and to what extent you are willing to commit your destiny to those beliefs. Remember, however, that it is precisely those beliefs
that make you a unique human being; and when you find
yourself in a position of leadership, respect for the beliefs
of others will mark you as a rare leader to be highly valued
by those who work under your direction. In order to help

you in clarifying your own values, the following exercise should be most instructive for you.

Values Clarification Questionnaire

		Agree	Disagree
1.	Money is very important to my happiness.	⎯	⎯
2.	I would rather have security than have a life of adventure.	⎯	⎯
3.	I would rather be respected and admired than be rich.	⎯	⎯
4.	I believe in equality for all, even though we're not all created equal.	⎯	⎯
5.	Being independent is much more important than making a lot of money.	⎯	⎯
6.	The United States should have a strong national defense.	⎯	⎯
7.	More public money should be poured into programs such as welfare, national health care, care for the elderly, etc.	⎯	⎯
8.	Cheating on my income tax is okay because the government isn't honest.	⎯	⎯
9.	I believe in the motto, "A day's work for a day's pay."	⎯	⎯
10.	Most crime is a result of poverty, not of bad character.	⎯	⎯

If you answer the above questionnaire as honestly as you can, you'll have some good beginning insights into your beliefs and your values. You'll quickly become conscious of the things that you prize most and value least in life, and this will go a long way in making you aware of the style that you should have. Polonius' advice to Laertes, "To thine own self be true, and it must follow as the night the day, thou canst not then be false to any man,"[4] rings as true today as it did 400 years ago. There are no "right" or "wrong" values. Those who hold values not in agreement with our own values may seem to be "wrong" to us; that is just not true. Therefore, we must make ourselves sensitive to the differences between ourselves and others; between ourselves and the organizations that we work for. We must develop sensitivity and awareness to the values that others prize most. This brings us to our third rule: *Analyze and know your own value system. It is what makes you unique. Become sensitive to the values that others prize.*

Environment

This is the fourth and final ingredient in making your style. The environment of your organization will be a strong conditioning factor for your style. In effect, the style of your organization will have a lot to do with how you articulate your thoughts, and how well you express your own individualism. Obviously, an organization that is run despotically will put quite a crimp in anyone's attempt to exercise individual style. An organization in which there is a lot of tradition or a strongly entrenched hierarchy with a chain of command that would make the Army top brass envious would also tend to suffocate the individual's style. What you must keep in mind is that the time will come when you will be able to express your individualism, and the sooner you become aware of the unique qualities that you have, the sooner you can put them to work for you, because as a manager you will be able to play an important role in changing the way in which your organization behaves; hence you'll be able to bring about changes in the style of your organization. It is important not to let your environment overwhelm you, or let it make such a strong impression on you that you become rigid and cannot do anything except by the company manual. Remember the adage, "He who lives by the book shall also perish by the book." Environments are important because they teach us different concepts and different approaches to problems. But never make the mistake of believing that all environments are the same or that what was expected of you by one organization will also be expected of you by another organization. In short, no two environments are the same, yet each will contribute a bit to the molding of our style.

EVEN FISH SWIM UPSTREAM

A sailboat fights the wind and the current to make headway; fish swim upstream over incredible obstacles so that they can spawn; and the nonconformist has to fight tradition, entrenched authority, and prejudice so that his voice and ideas can be heard. But it's the nonconformists who advance the world. The traditionalists who refuse to change may impede progress temporarily, but they will soon go the way of the dinosaurs. It's the innovators—the people with new and refreshing ideas—who are the wave of the future. So don't be afraid to be different; pity those who are afraid to break out of the shell of conformity. They will not have as much fun or success from life as you will.

But to what extent can you be "different?" How far can you go in developing your uniqueness? And to what extent can you advertise yourself as a nonconformist thinker who comes up with original ideas? These are all legitimate questions that can be asked by the novice leader.

First, one does not become different simply for the sake of self-advertisement. Building a reputation as a person who strives to be as contrary as possible is certainly not the answer. You develop your style because that's what your temperament and personality are best attuned to. Your style is the product of your personality, and it will be shaped and molded into your style by your interaction with peers, subordinates, and even the competition. For example, your makeup may lead you to become an innovator—one who is always looking to perform a job in a more efficient, less expensive way. By constantly looking for ways to improve performance, you can quickly earn a reputation as an innovative leader. Or you may have the personality and temperament of the charismatic leader. That is, one who can inspire subordinates and even peers to excel in their performance. This requires great skill in handling people, and you can quickly earn an enviable reputation as one who can get the most out of the people who work for you. Perhaps your major asset is an eye for detail. You can easily build a reputation here that will make you indispensable. Perhaps you are a creative person who likes to experiment with new ideas or new products. Here again, there is great opportunity in store for you. You may be a person who is able to lead by teamwork. In this case, you could easily develop some new approaches perhaps to productivity; and a few experiments in this area could quickly demonstrate that you are a valuable manager indeed.

The few examples above are clues to the manner in which you will be able to stand out as a nonconformist—an individualist who can think for himself—as well as a person who has a great deal to contribute to the organization.

The first step is to discover your own temperament and personality. Get yourself psychologically tested if you have to. The next step is to work at developing those unique traits of yours. You'll not only be happy expressing those traits; you'll be successful as well. Our fourth rule, then, is: *Do not become a nonconformist because it's the "smart" thing to do. Exploit your best traits and talents and use them to show that you can make a unique contribution. That is the proper exercise of nonconformity.*

SUMMARY

The day of the organization man is over. The corporate clone has been found to be wanting. Instead, organizations are realizing the value of having individualists who can think for themselves as their managers.

Nonconformity extracts a higher price from the individual, but it also provides greater rewards. Nonconformity means that there will be more conflict, but from this conflict, creative energy will be released; hence, nonconformity is a healthy attribute for any organization to have. If it were not for nonconformists there would be little advancement in industry, business, or the professions.

There are many excellent examples of men who have defied tradition. Among these are Frederick Tudor, A. Ernest Fitzgerald, Henry J. Kaiser, and Alexander Dingee. Their business biographies prove that nonconformity knows neither time nor place, and that there is room for the person with an unusual idea in every age.

The successful manager has to know what kind of style he should adopt for himself, if he is to stand out from the rest of the crowd. For this reason, it is valuable to look at various personality studies of leadership types, so that we can gain insight into our own personalities. Five personality types (the craftsman, the jungle fighter, the company man, the gamesman, and the maverick) are compared and typed. In addition, four different kinds of character (active-positive, active-negative, passive-positive, and passive-negative) also are compared and contrasted.

Values are extremely important to the individualist. One must get to know oneself through the values that he prizes most. Clarification of values thus becomes an important tool that we can use in developing our style.

Environment is also crucial to our development, as we are molded by the kind of organizational environment that we find ourselves in. Personality, character, values, and environment are crucial to development of our individual styles. Each should be carefully thought about by any person aspiring to become a leader.

Finally, being different is not to be disparaged unless it's done because it's the thing to do. Being different has to be a carefully thought out process wherein the individual attempts to mold his style around his personality and character traits, and then proceeds to build a reputation based on what he most excels at.

The Four Rules of Nonconformity

1. Don't become a clone. Realize that nonconformity is at the root of all great endeavors.
2. Study the different character and personality types. Learn to analyze yourself as well as the people around you. Above all, learn to accommodate yourself by becoming complementary to those on whom your advancement depends.
3. Analyze and know your own value system. It is what makes you unique. Become sensitive to the values that others prize.
4. Do not become a nonconformist because it's the "smart" thing to do. Exploit your best traits and talents and use them to show that you can make a unique contribution. That is the proper exercise of nonconformity.

Exercises for Chapter Four

1. Values clarification
List three persons (they can be either famous or familiar):

(a) The person you would most want to be like.
(b) The person you would want most *not* to be like.
(c) The person you think is most like you.

For each person that you have named, what character or personality traits can you name that each has that you find repulsive? Which do you admire? Make a list of those traits under two columns: The first should be labeled, "Values I admire most in people"; the second should be labeled, "Values I admire least in people." These are a strong clue to the values that you hold. Finally, take a plain piece of paper and write on it the values that you think your organization has. Do they prize fair dealing? money? manipulation? honesty? List next the values that your superiors have. Do the values of your organization and those of your superiors match with yours? If so, you are in luck. If not, perhaps you are working in the wrong environment. Finally, read a book on values clarification, such as: *Values Clarification* by Simon, Howe, and Kirschenbaum, Hart Publishing Company, New York, 1972.

2. Personality types

Take 10 people whom you work with, and list the personality traits that identify them as belonging in the category of: Craftsman, jungle fighter, company man, gamesman, or maverick. Now indicate whom have been most successful in rising to the leadership. Who have been the happiest in their jobs? Who have made the most money? Who do you think that you are most like? Do the same for character types, i.e. active-positive, active-negative, etc.

3. Innovation

Make a list of 10 innovations that you would like to see your organization make. How would you justify making these innovations? How would you go about trying to implement them?

NOTES

1. Michael Maccoby, *The Gamesman.* Simon & Schuster, New York, 1976.

2. Robert N. McMurry, *The Maverick Executive.* AMACOM, New York, 1974. pp. 11–15.

3. James David Barber, *Presidential Character.* Prentice-Hall, Englewood Cliffs, N.J., 1977. pp. 12–13.

4. William Shakespeare, *Hamlet,* Act I, sc. iii.

5

Timing

The Pregnancy of Time

Imagine that you are on a train. You are headed from point A to point B. With each passing second, the distance behind you grows longer, while the distance before you grows shorter as you approach your destination. Yet, you are sitting on the train, all the while as though on some stationary object. Only the click-clack of the wheels and the swaying motion of the train give you any feeling of motion. You look at your watch. Each minute seems to pass slowly, as you anxiously await your arrival at point B. Which time seems shorter? The time that you left behind? Or the time yet ahead of you? Conversely, which seems longer? Does the time you are spending on the train seem to be the longest? Are you anxious to reach your destination? Or are you looking back longingly at the place you left behind?

Many years ago, H. G. Wells wrote a science fiction novel, *The Time Machine.*[1] Let us now imagine that instead of being on board a train, we are on board H. G.

Wells' marvelous time machine, going from 1945 to the year 2000. The wonderful thing about that miraculous time machine was that it could be stopped in the present; it could move its passenger into the future, many millenia away; or it could be reversed to travel into the past as well. If you were a traveller aboard that time machine, in which direction would you want to go? Where would you place yourself on the scale of time?

Now for a surprise! You already have a time machine; it's in your head. How you perceive time, and how you relate to time depends a great deal on your time "sense." Not all of us relate to time in the same way; some of us want to travel in reverse to the good old days of nostalgia; others are content to go wherever the time machine will take us, as long as we remain in the "eternal" present. Still others want to get the machine in gear and head into the future as quickly as possible. Obviously, not all of us are the same in the way in which we think about time; and as this will have a great deal to do with the way in which we shape our careers, it is important to think for a while on what kind of time sense we have, and how we can develop a better appreciation of time and that finest of all arts, *timing*. There are three kinds of time that bear a close look. These are: *past time, present time,* and *future time.* Let's look at what each means to us.

Past Time

Shakespeare's admonition, "What's past is Prologue," is still quite true. As our future is gobbled up by the passage of time, the past grows rapidly and swells to fill the memory banks in our brains. In fact, it can be said that all we really have is our past, for our future is not yet to be and our present recedes so quickly that it becomes our past in the momentary flick of an eyelash. All of our memories, all of our experiences—good and bad—are buried in our past, and we can only learn how to behave in the future from our past mistakes and triumphs. However, most of us do not see our past in the same way. Remembering that our

scale of time reads from 1945 to 2000, place yourself on
that time scale, in the present. Now let's move our time
machine backwards. What periods of your life are most
important to you? What periods were the most pleasant?
Which were the most unpleasant? Which were the most
creative? Which provided the greatest job satisfaction?
The events and circumstances that appear to have been
the most important for you will stand out in bas-relief
against the time scale, and it will soon be evident how you
see yourself by looking at your past. Another important
clue is to discover which time of your past was most pleasant; that is, most filled with pleasant memories. If those
pleasant memories go into the remote past, you are the
kind of person who concentrates on the remote past, and
thus may be quite dissatisfied with the recent past, 10 or
15 years ago, for example. Or, conversely, if you are more
concerned about the recent past, you are probably repress-
ing unpleasant memories about your remote past. One
simple way to determine what your past orientation is, is
to write down the most important events of your life. When
did they occur? If they occurred during the first third of
your past life, you are living more in the remote past than
in the recent past. Probably you have found the remote
past to be a more pleasant place than the recent past or
even the present. Now you should examine the recent past
because even though you don't like to think about it, there
is much to be learned from it.

Take the last two thirds of your past life. Write down the
important events in two columns headed "good" and
"bad." You should really make two lists: one for your career and one for your personal or social life. Try to list as
many events as you can. Do they reflect a sense of winning? of achievement? of independence? of resentment? of
failure? of adversity? By analyzing your recent past and by
discovering what kinds of things were most important to
you, you will be able to guide your own future career more
intelligently. No person can have good timing if he or she
does not have some sense of what has happened in the past
and of how he or she looks at those events. From the inven-

tory that you have taken from your memory banks, you now have a much clearer idea of what has been important to you and what kinds of mistakes you may have made in the past. We cannot have a clear idea of where we are going if we do not know where we have been.

Present Time

The present is squeezed in somewhere between the past and the future. In a sense there really is no present, for in an instant all that was present is now past. So, we speak of a "present" in the psychological, not the chronological, sense. As the future is about to become part of the present, so is the present about to become part of the past. But this does not answer the problem, "What about my present?" The answer to this question really lies within you.

There is a technique that is widely used nowadays in movies and television. It is the technique of "freezing" a still image on the screen for a few seconds or longer. This gives us the image of a still photograph, and we come away with a strong impression of that momentary action or expression on the faces of the actors. Yet freezing is also distortion and really takes the image out of the normal contexts of space and time in which the rest of the action is framed. In a sense, some of us also "freeze" the present to the point that we distort our sense of continuity and proportion.

How, then, do you see your present? Do you think of it as being longer than a day? a week? a year? Or do you think of it as being extremely brief? For how long do you "freeze" your present?

If you think of yourself as being in a "present" time frame that lasts for about a week at a time, you are probably average. Most people think of the present time of their lives in terms of from a week to a month's duration. If you think of your present time as a day or less, you are probably a person who is anxiously awaiting the future; in fact, you can hardly wait to get there. If your present seems to be extraordinarily dreary and drawn out, you are probably a person who has enjoyed life in the past much more than in the present.

Another clue as to how you regard the present is to ask yourself which days of the week you favor most. Traditionally, "Blue Monday" and "Thank goodness it's Friday!" have become national ritual jokes. But are they really jokes? What do they tell you about your attitudes toward your work responsibilities? To discover your own attitudes, make a list of the days of the week on a piece of paper. Grade them from 1 to 7, with 1 being the day of the week that you like most, and 7 being the day of the week that you least enjoy. If you liked Monday least, you are probably in excellent company, as that day seems to fulfill almost a universal feeling of dread. In fact, time and motion study experts have indicated that not only do certain hours of the day but certain days of the week show lower productivity and more mistakes than other days; and Mondays and Fridays are the chief culprits. It used to be an accepted *caveat* that if you bought an automobile that was assembled on a Monday, you were almost certain to get a lemon.

If you liked Saturdays and Sundays best, chances are that you are enjoying your leisure time more than your working time. If you liked weekdays better, chances are that you enjoy your work, and you are looking forward to getting back into the swing of things. Now try one more small test. Write down the word "present." Below it, write down the period of time that the word present signifies to you. If it is a year or more, there is a strong chance that you find yourself tied much more to the past than to the future; hence, you tend to find more satisfaction and reward in your past than in your future possibilities. Perhaps it is time to give serious thought to your career and your job. In general, the briefer the span of time that you think is occupied by the present, the more future oriented you are, and the more impatient you are for the work week with its subsequent train of events to occur.

That time machine in your head, your brain, thus sees the passage of time as relative to the manner in which you pass the time available to you. For some of us, time literally stands still like the frozen images on television or in the movies. For others, it flies by so quickly that we soon feel like some poor, helpless creature watching the ceaseless grinding of the huge wheels of time. How you look at time is also part of how you look at life, and since you spend most of it working, we are really talking about how you look at your working life. If the days, weeks, months, etc. drag by so slowly that you give little thought to the future, perhaps you should take a closer look at your life and your goals.

Future Time

Let's return for a few moments to the train on which you were traveling from point A to point B. You could choose several places to be on that train. You might be on the rear observation platform, watching the world recede from you as your train traveled forward; or you could be seated in the middle of the train, looking out of the side window as the train neared its future destination; or you could be seated somewhere up front where the engineer sits, considering only what lies ahead of you. Remember, no matter where you are on our mythical train, you are still moving forward. The question is, are you looking backward at the same time, watching the past recede with some regret (and perhaps some confusion)? Or are you peering ahead, anxious to see what's around the next bend in the road? Perhaps you are content merely to be traveling into the future with only a sidelong glance at the passing landscape to make sure that that's where you are headed. Where we are on the train has a great deal to do with how we look at future time.

As a manager, you will have to learn to live much more in the future than in the past, so it's a good idea to think of yourself as sitting up in the front of that train with the engineer. In other words, you must become future oriented and acquire the sensitivity to be able to anticipate the developments that will occur in the future. Most intelligent people give at least some thought to the future. That's why they buy houses, take out pension plans, or save money. But these kinds of activities of themselves do not indicate an ability to anticipate the future. There is a great difference between *fear* of the future and *awareness* of the future. It is precisely that difference that separates the astute and the intelligent from the people who are victims of their own fantasies and anxieties. Thinking about the future is not easy. It requires insight, education, and time. But it is quite rewarding, and as we shall see later on, you simply cannot make any headway in life unless you are willing to give plenty of thought and attention to future planning. Since timing, to be successful, requires a confluence of events that will take place some time in the future, we are simply not meeting the requirements of good timing if we do not pay attention to where we are going and why.

Therefore, you have to begin thinking about the road ahead of that mythical time train that you are on. You are always moving forward, but do you give any thought to what kinds of conditions you will find when you arrive at your destination? How far ahead do you plan your own life? What will you be doing 5 years from now? 10 years? 20 years? How well you face the future depends heavily upon how much you can learn about it; this requires the development of insights and becoming a more informed person. If you want to ride up front with the engineer, you'll have to know almost as much as he does!

Ever since man first appeared on this planet, he has been concerned about the passage of time. The early development of instruments for measuring time stands as testimony to this concern. History is also a good teacher when we look at ancient civilizations. Those civilizations that became too preoccupied with their past glories forgot that they had a future to worry about, and they soon passed into dust. Similarly, those organizations (and their managers) who try to live in the past will soon be unable to cope with the challenges that the future will surely present them with. Included below are a number of interesting quotations about time that reflect human concern with this problem. They have been carefully selected to serve as guideposts for you.[2]

All my possessions for a moment of time!

> Queen Elizabeth I on her deathbed

The reason I beat the Austrians is that they did not know the value of five minutes.

> Napoleon

We sleep, but the loom of time never stops and the pattern which was weaving when the sun went down is weaving when it comes up in the morning.

> Henry Ward Beecher

They who await no gifts from Chance have conquered Fate.

> Matthew Arnold

Each is given a bag of tools,
A shapeless mass,
A book of rules;
And each must make
Ere life is flown
A stumbling block
Or a stepping stone

> R. L. Sharpe

To choose time is to save time; and an unseasonable motion is but beating the air.

> Sir Francis Bacon

The present is big with the future.

> Leibnitz

He who rests, rots.

> Arthur Fiedler

Procrastination is the thief of time.

> Edward Young

The future is purchased by the present.

> Samuel Johnson

The mill cannot grind with the water that is past.

> Sarah Doudney

We shall never have any more time. We have, and always had all the time there is.

Arnold Bennett

By the street of "By and By" one arrives at the house of "Never."

Cervantes

Know the true value of time; snatch, seize and enjoy every moment of it. No idleness; no laziness; no procrastination; never put off till tomorrow what you can do today.

Lord Chesterfield

All things come to him who waits—provided he knows what he is waiting for.

Woodrow Wilson

Today is the first day of the rest of your life.

Anonymous

Our first rule, then, is: *Learn the value of time, and learn how you relate to the past, the present, and the future.*

OPPORTUNITY RIVER

We all live on the banks of Opportunity River. Some of us are content to sit and watch the river flow by our door, while others are anxious to immerse themselves in its waters. Every time that we "get our feet wet" we are subjecting ourselves to new experiences and new opportunities. However, we cannot continually immerse ourselves; we must come up for air and look around. Moreover, there are periods when it would be unwise or even unhealthy for us to immerse ourselves. Therefore, we have to become choosy and plan when we are going to jump in; and when we are going to content ourselves with staying on the river bank and contemplating the flow of the current.

Timing is a fine art, but it can be learned and used judiciously as long as you are willing to follow and apply a few basic rules. The first basic rule is in the shape of a formula: $\frac{O \times P}{T} = M$. This formula can best be understood in the following terms. O stands for opportunity; P stands for possibilities; T stands for time; M stands for move. A good way to remember it is *OPT to Move.* To explain further, opportunities are nothing in themselves if there are no possibilities; and possibilities are simply not attainable if the factor of time is not taken into consideration. Time thus becomes the great divisor that forces us to condition ourselves to the expediency of time. The problem of knowing when to play out our *OPTion to Move* can thus best be illustrated by the following example:

> Harry S. has been an assistant sales manager at the XYZ Corporation for the past 3 years. He has been doing such a good job that another corporation has approached him and has offered him the position of sales manager at a salary increase of $5,000 per year. Should Harry move? Perhaps, but in order to make his decision wisely, Harry should make some careful investigations and do some thoughtful review before he makes any decision. Five thousand dollars and a promotion is very tempting, but it can still lead Harry down the wrong road.

What are some of the facts that Harry has to consider? These are the same facts that you will have to consider when Opportunity River beckons to you. It may or may not be the time to step into it. These are also rules for achieving a better sense of timing. So let's take a look at some of the rules for OPTing (opportunity timing) that Harry should use in making his decision.

Rule 1. Does the opportunity that presents itself mesh with your long-range plans? That is, can you see how this new position would fit into the plans that you have already made for your own career? In Harry's case, he is quite happy at the thought of being a sales manager. In fact, he can imagine himself as being quite comfortable in the job, and sees himself as being able to advance to vice president after he has proven himself as sales manager.

Rule 2. What are the long-range possibilities of the opportunity presenting itself? What are the short-range possibilities? Perhaps Harry has already considered both possibilities, but chances are he hasn't. To do this properly, you will have to take both perspectives separately, and try to plot out where this new job will lead in a 5-year period. To do this, you would have to have information about the growth of the company, its present status, and the reputation of the people who manage it. Check it out to see if it has a bad or good name among its competitors. How about its customers? How do they feel about the company? What are its growth prospects? How much do you think *you* will be able to grow with them? How does the company compare with the company that you are now working for? Finally, the acid test! Would you be willing to go to work for them if it meant taking a cut in pay? If the answer is yes, chances are that the opportunity is presenting itself to you as a chance to grow; and if the money involved is only secondary, this means that the growth benefits are the primary consideration. Harry has considered this aspect carefully, and has come to the conclusion that he wouldn't take the job if it meant a cut in salary. So apparently, he doesn't feel that this opportunity means enough growth to justify his moving.

Rule 3. What is the time frame context within which the opportunity is presenting itself? Is the time frame the same as *your* time frame? That is, does it fit in with the period of time in which you expected to be in that particular slot in life? Or are you running ahead of schedule? Running ahead of schedule can, in some ways, be as bad as running behind schedule. Many a good career was ruined because the individual took the job before he or she was ready for it. If the time frame differential is too great, exercise caution before you make any major changes. Remember that job-hopping does not look too good on your record either. So you must weigh the opportunity against your readiness in terms of time for it. In the case of Harry S., he came to the conclusion that the opportunity came along a little too early in his career and that he had not yet built up enough of a track record with his present firm to be impressive enough a few years down the road, even though his company's competition was impressed enough with him to offer Harry a better paying and more responsible position.

Rule 4. What are the environmental conditions? When you decide to jump into Opportunity River, you swim alone, and you may have to fight the current as well. The river can run swiftly—too swiftly—in some cases, and you'll find yourself in difficulty. To assess any new opportunity, you must weigh the environmental factors. The internal environment of the company that wants your services should be carefully examined by you. Perhaps you could talk to ex-employees about conditions there. Or perhaps you could talk discreetly to people who work there presently. Sometimes a company's customers are a good source of information about what's going on inside an organization. At any rate, a careful investigation of the internal environment is well-advised because moving to the other company without considering the internal environment could result in personal tragedy and misery for you. The external environment is just as important as well. What kind of a track record does the company have? What has been the record of its earnings? Its stock market position? Its financial standing? What about the market conditions? What kinds of economic problems does it face? What will a change in certain economic conditions (the money market, the energy crisis, etc.) do to the prospects of the organization? Is it in good financial health? Do the very best that you can to answer all of these questions. The president may drive a Rolls Royce and live in a $500,000 house, but the company could easily be on the way out. In Harry's case, he saw that the company that offered him the position was number two in the market, directly behind the company that he worked for. Harry felt that the competition was good and that the firm that wanted him had a good chance to become number one. Moreover, Harry investigated the internal power structure and found that it was the kind of organization that he would be comfortable in. So Harry decided that from the environmental point of view the new opportunity, although a risk, was encouraging and promised to become a place where Harry would grow.

Rule 5. What are the possibilities for advancement where you are now? Do not rule these out altogether. While you may not receive immediate satisfaction, you must consider the possibilities of your present environment. In Harry's case, he knew the sales manager intimately. He was convinced that the sales manager was not about to move. Moreover, the vice president's slot was also taken by a very good man who probably wouldn't be moving either in the foreseeable future. Harry was forced to come to the conclusion that there was no reason to believe that things would change much for him over the next 5 years, and he had already been with the same firm for 3 years. Thus Harry's conclusion on rule 5 would be that it's a good idea to move, because mobility in his present environment would be extremely slow.

Rule 6. What will you gain by moving? What will you lose? What are the advantages? the disadvantages? For this, Harry drew up a chart of gains and losses. The "breaking-in" period could be most difficult; on the other hand, Harry had better get used to new situations. After all, that's what being an executive is all about. Perhaps he would grow considerably as a result. Harry came to the conclusion that he would stand to gain more than he would lose by moving.

Now let's go back and review Harry's decision whether or not to step into Opportunity River at this time. Rule 1 dealt with Harry's long-range plans. He had to agree that his personal long-range plans meshed well with the opportunity. Rule 2 dealt with the long-range possibilities of growth for Harry. Harry reluctantly came to the conclusion that his possibilities for growth in the new firm were really no better than in his present environment. Rule 3 dealt with Harry's time frame (time schedule). Harry concluded that the opportunity had come along a little too early in his career. He didn't want to be a "job-hopper."

Rule 4 dealt with the environmental conditions of the firm that offered Harry the job. He concluded that the firm had an encouraging external as well as internal environment. Rule 5 indicated that Harry's mobility might be extremely limited if he stayed where he was. Thus, Harry felt that moving would speed up his chances for advancement. Rule 6 dealt with the gains and losses that Harry would have if he moved. Actually, in sum, Harry's analysis showed that there were only two major drawbacks to deciding to move to the new firm now. One was that he already was working for the leader, and long-range prospects did not show any significant change in position for either firm. The other reason was that such a plan to move did not fit in well with Harry's time frame. What did Harry decide to do? He decided to take the job, but more money was not the chief factor in his decision. As you can see, there were many more important factors to be considered, and Harry had to weigh each of them carefully. Timing is a delicate art, and must be the product of intelligent deliberation. Opportunity River can be very fickle indeed. It can speed you on to a successful career, or it can trap you in the whirlpool of disaster. Many a person who has made a hasty move has bemoaned his fate later. That's too late to cry. A little intelligent foresight and investigation could easily help you avoid such tragedies. Don't be overwhelmed by offers of money. Investigate your own motivations and be sure that the new position, whether you go after it or it goes after you, is really what you want and really will offer you the kind of growth that you are looking for. It was the challenge of growth that made Harry accept the new job.

The same six rules for determining whether Opportunity River really is beckoning to you with something worthwhile will also work for internal situations. That is, opportunities can be just as worthwhile within your organization as anything that might be offered or available outside. Your possibilities for advancement from within should not be overlooked.

One of the great difficulties about seeking to advance from within an organization, however, is fear. Fear that you are not well known; fear that the opening you seek will not open up for a long time; fear that moving upward will cause you all kinds of problems with those who have worked with you and perhaps will become resentful of your success. And, of course, there is always the fear that your new superiors and co-workers will be constantly measuring you against the kind of job performance that you had before. None of these problems are present when a fresh start is being made in a strange, new, and sometimes exciting situation with a new organization, but they'll crop up there in time as well!

At any rate, there are also some positive factors to be considered in staying with your present organization. The first is a sense of security that comes from being with the same people in the same organization. Have you ever noticed how important executives always take some of their top people with them when they move to a new organization? They do this primarily to feel secure; their old friends (cronies?) provide a sort of protective armor for them and insulate them from the shock and terrors of being completely surrounded in a new, unfamiliar situation. Top executives are only human also! Nevertheless, your knowledge of the firm you are connected with, its inner workings, its history, its policy, and the kind of loyalty that you probably feel for it, will all be difficult to break away from. So think it over carefully, and remember that Opportunity River flows right through your firm's backyard as well as by your house.

Finally, it is important to bear in mind that opportunity, like lightning, never strikes twice in the same place. There is a hackneyed old saying, "history repeats itself," which is about the most misleading piece of nonsense ever concocted. Human nature may have its limits and thus be repetitive, but history repeating itself? Never! Time and new conditions change all that frequently. Opportunity likewise will never repeat itself in exactly the same way again. That does not mean, of course, that there won't be any new opportunities. What it does mean is that each new opportunity is a unique one, and must be considered in that light. An opportunity once passed up will never present itself again in exactly the same way.

Over 500 years before the birth of Christ, there was a group of Greek philosophers and scientists who understood as well as any modern man the meaning of the passage of time. One of them, Anaximander, said: "It is necessary that things should pass away into that from which they are born. For things must pay one another the penalty and compensation for their injustice according to the ordinance of time."[3] Anaximander understood as well as any human being that there is motion as well as meaning in life, and that the flowing river of time (opportunity) will never cease its perpetual motion. Anaximander had another philosopher friend who also understood the uniqueness of opportunity. Thales deciphered old Babylonian astronomical charts and successfully predicted a drought for the olive trees. He begged and borrowed enough money to corner that year's olive crop and established a monopoly for himself. Legend has it that he was correct and made a fortune! If ancient peoples could understand the meaning of time and opportunity, then we moderns had better pay some attention. Our second rule, then, is: *Whenever Opportunity River beckons, be circumspect. Don't jump in without looking. Remember, it won't beckon twice in the same way.*

SIX RULES

1. Keep your career goals in mind.
2. Examine long and short-range possibilities.
3. Be sure you are in the same time frame as your opportunity.
4. Examine the environmental conditions carefully.
5. Reexamine your present position.
6. Carefully list the advantages and disadvantages.

WHERE DID THE TIME GO?

That is a question that we always ask ourselves. There never seems to be enough time in a busy day to get everything done. The greatest complaint that executives have is that they lack time. A study by Henry Mintzberg[4] indicates that executives spend most of their verbal contact hours as follows:

Giving and receiving information	40 percent
Decision making	21 percent
Filling requests	18 percent
Ceremonial, organizational work	21 percent

Mintzberg's study also indicates that from 60 to 80 percent of a manager's time was taken up by one kind of verbal contact or another. Most manager's jobs, Mintzberg points out, are characterized by three factors: variety, brevity, and fragmentation. That is, executives experience a great deal of diversity in their work; much of it is in short bursts rather than in prolonged sessions; and the work they do tends to be more of a piecemeal nature, often interrupted, and frequently without any final resolution.

Thus, the manager has to play a sort of continual juggling act, trying his best to manage his activities within the amount of time allotted him. Mintzberg also studied the amount of time allotted by executives to daily activities, and this is also interesting to look at:

Total Percentage of Time Allocation by Executives

Unscheduled Meetings	10 percent
Tours	3 percent
Desk work	22 percent
Telephone calls	6 percent
Scheduled meetings	59 percent

Obviously, meetings and desk work took up the greatest share of time of the average executive's schedule. Verbal activity is what eats up most of the time and energy of the managerial executive, and is where he has to exercise the greatest caution. Using time in the most efficient and expedient manner possible is the mark of the successful executive. There is an old saying, "If you want to get something done, find a busy man." Precisely because busy people have to be better organized, they learn to manage their time better and can accomplish much more than many who have all the time in the world on their hands and yet seem to accomplish nothing. There are a number of guidelines that can be followed, and they will undoubtedly result in better time management for you than you ever dreamed possible.

The first step in achieving better time management is to take an *inventory*. Before you can use your time more efficiently, you have to find out how you are using it now. Your time inventory should cover every minute of each working day, including such items as telephone time, lunch breaks or other breaks, time spent reading and answering mail, and time spent in meetings or whatever miscellaneous time you might be spending in relation to your job. If you have to take work home or attend social functions that are related to your job, you should inventory those as well. Now that we have a handle on where the time is going we can proceed with the diagnosis.

The next step is in making a correct *diagnosis* of where you are spending your time, and of trying to take the proper measures to correct time-wasting. An inventory and diagnosis of where and how time was spent could easily result in finding as much as 3 extra hours in every day. And a lot can be done in those 3 hours.

Following the diagnosis, there are a number of interesting guidelines that are observed by most successful executives:

(a) What are your greatest time wasters? Do you spend too much time on trivia? Are you doing things that are not important to your function? Are there any activities that you could omit altogether that would not cause any harm to your job?

(b) How many of your activities could be delegated to someone else without causing any harm to your function as manager? Could you eliminate any telephone calls? any interviews? Instead of answering every letter, could you delegate the job to your secretary? Are some meetings a waste of time for you? Why not send a subordinate instead, and you could spend your time in a more valuable way. These days, travel becomes especially burdensome in terms of the amounts of valuable time that will be used up.

(c) How well organized are the meetings that you have to have? As we have already seen, meetings and conferences take up more than a third of the average executive's time. But they can become endlessly wasteful unless they are properly organized and get to the point very quickly. A meeting can easily degenerate into a "bull session." Therefore, successful tactics for meetings have to be used. An agenda should be prepared and the participants required to stick to it. Each participant in the meeting should come prepared so there's no time wasted fumbling for papers and reports. In fact, it's a good idea to create some internal discipline in a meeting by setting a time limit on each participant. You will soon be amazed at how much more people can say in less time, once they have learned to organize their thinking and their preparation.

(d) Avoid frenetic activities. These are usually precipitated by some kind of crisis. To be sure, there always have been and always will be crises to contend with, but keeping them to a minimum by the use of foresight and wise planning will prove to be a great conserver of time for you. The principal reason that crisis is such a great time waster is that it interrupts all of the other processes. All of the wheels have to be stopped while the crisis is resolved. Then everyone tries to pick up the pieces and resume their normal activities. Such breaks in the normal, routine flow of activity are bound to have a deleterious effect on both the morale and the time usage of any executive. If your time diagnosis indicates to you that there is a great deal of time spent on dealing with crisis-related activities, something is radically wrong and you should take remedial action.

(e) Try to create some big blocks of time that you can use for creative thinking and planning activities. After all, as an executive, you're being paid to come up with innovative ideas, and to find cheaper, easier, and more effective ways of doing things. If that's true, you need periods of quiet time, when you can devote some uninterrupted time and attention to long-range problems and creative thinking. A moment here or there or having to do creative thinking in bed just before one falls asleep or when one is too tired to really give it his or her best is not the answer.

(f) Practice time consolidation. A very successful executive I know uses the technique of consolidation or "bunching" and thus finds that he can save a great deal of time. Answering phone calls only at certain hours or dictating letters only at certain times can be a lifesaver. The same could be said for interviewing people or for holding conferences. The time pie is only so large. The more we can cram into one segment, the more room that is left in the other segments.

As an executive, you owe it to your organization as well as to yourself to make the best possible use of your time, and to allow enough discretionary time for creative activity that will help your organization prosper. Careful handling of time is as important as careful handling of money. As Peter Drucker points out,[5]

Effective executives, in my observation, do not start with their tasks. They start with their time. And they do not start out with planning. They start by finding out where their time actually goes. Then they attempt to manage their time and to cut back unproductive demands on their time. Finally they consolidate their "discretionary" time into the largest possible continuing units.

One final point. You should become well acquainted with your own biological clock. Planning time schedules should closely coincide with the executive's own preferences. Otherwise, he will not be able to give it his best. If he is a "morning" person, then that is the best time of day to tackle more difficult jobs. If he is an "afternoon" person, more demanding work should be put off until then if possible. Our third rule, then, is: *Audit your own time expenditures closely and prepare a schedule that will maximize your most efficient use of time.*

A Man with a Plan

Change is the only real constant in our environment. We all live with it and absorb it daily in what we read, see, hear, and encounter. Yet, much of the change that surrounds us never really registers. Instead, it slowly surrounds us until it overwhelms us, and one day, we awaken to find that the world has suddenly changed. Shocked, we think to ourselves, "What a dirty trick life has played on me. And here I was thinking that things would go on forever as they were." So most of us are shocked by an energy shortage, or by the changing status of the dollar, or by inflation, or by all kinds of new conditions that somehow seemed to have blossomed within the past 24 hours. Not even enough time to catch your breath!

The human organism is remarkably adaptable. One would think that with all this change going on, mankind would be so shell shocked that he would be afraid or incapable of continuing his daily activities. Yet continue he does. And so it is with most of us. We acquire battle scars, but we pick ourselves up, brush off the dirt, and somehow devise a new plan to cope with the latest crisis. Some of us even find a way to profit from the latest crisis.

Unfortunately, while all this change is going on around us, and while we are even willing to adapt to these new changes, we tend to stand in place while new ideas and new developments are swirling around us. How often have you heard people say, "If I could predict what's going to happen, I would be a millionaire!" What these people are saying is that it's impossible to cope with the future, so they give up trying. But not being able to cope with the future is *not* the mark of a leader. Leadership is essentially characterized by the ability to develop and use foresight. As you are going to be a successful leader, so you will also develop and use your foresight both in personal life and in your career. All of the great business leaders and industrialists have this remarkable ability, which is most often described as a "gift." It wasn't a gift. It was the application of intelligence and perception to foresee the future from the conditions of the present. Now let's find out how you can determine your future.

Take the number "70." That will represent the maximum working age that you can hope to achieve. Few people go on past that age, at least under present conditions. Now write down your present age. Subtract it from 70. This is the number of years that you have left at the maximum, provided that death, illness, or other catastrophes do not intervene. It has often been said that most men and women achieve their maximum levels of development and achievement during their late 40s and early to middle 50s. If that is true, then the 12 years from age 58 to 70, for example, are "downhill." Thus, it is imperative that you take advantage of the "uphill" stage of your life, and plan for a future that will bring you to the fruitful stage of your career in full bloom. This will take both planning and foresight. Thus, from your present age to that point of maximum development that we just described as age 58, you should begin to mark off the future stages of your working life. Make it a point to set goals. Try to analyze where you think you'd like to be. Getting there is only half the battle. Finding out where to go is the other half. Many successful men and women have planned out their careers as a general would plan out a battle. It's up to you to develop your own sense of timing, and prepare your own battle plan for the future. You will be well rewarded for it.

Summary

Most of us spend little energy thinking about time; hence we do not develop any sensitivity to time, and we give little thought to planning our future. There are three kinds of time that we must become sensitive to if we are going to be able to do any rational planning for the future. These three kinds of time are: past time, present time, and future time. Placing these three kinds of time in proper perspective will help develop your goals, and also help you to understand yourself better.

Opportunity River indicates that opportunities are always around us. The problem is when to attempt to jump into that river, and when to choose the wiser course, and stay out of the river because we may not be ready for the river yet. One way to learn whether or not we are ready for new opportunities is by testing our possibilities against the six rules of "OPTing to move."

As a leader, the one important thing you will have to learn will be to use your time to the best advantage. This means that you must diagnose what you do with the time you have, and then try to diagnose what's wrong with the way you spend your time now. Can you put your time to more profitable use? Inventory, analysis, diagnosis, and remedy are the chief keys to developing more successful time management.

Finally, you must take the time that you have left to you in your career, and make the most of it. this means that you must live in the present and the future, and become adaptable to the everchanging conditions of the world. In other words, you must become future oriented if you are to be a worthy leader.

The Three Rules of Good Timing

1. Learn the value of time, and learn how you relate to the past, the present, and the future.

2. Whenever Opportunity River beckons, be circumspect. Don't jump in without looking. Pay attention to the six rules:

   (a) Keep your career goals in mind.
   (b) Examine long-range and short-range possibilities.
   (c) Be sure you are in the same time frame as your opportunity.
   (d) Examine the environmental conditions carefully.
   (e) Reexamine your present position.
   (f) Make a careful list of the advantages and disadvantages. Only then can you make a decision.

3. Audit your own expenditures of time closely, and prepare a schedule that will maximize your most efficient use of time.

EXERCISES FOR CHAPTER 5

1. Construct your own time chart. Mark off every 5 years, from age 0 to age 70. For time already spent, list important events. From your present age to 70, list events that are likely to happen. Example:

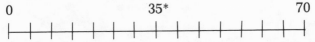

0   35*   70

2. Time flow and inventory. Prepare a chart showing exactly how you spend each minute of every day. Keep this chart for a 2-week period, and then take a daily average of exactly where and how you spend your time.

3. Make a list of all of the good opportunities that you would like to see come your way in the future. When would you like them to come your way? What is your time frame? Refer to the chart in exercise 1.

*Present age

4. Read *Future Shock* by Alvin Toffler.
5. Read *Passages* by Gail Sheehy.

NOTES

1. H. G. Wells, *The Time Machine.* Bantam Books Inc., New York, 1968.

2. Godfrey M. Lebhar, *The Use of Time,* 3rd ed. Chain Store Publishing Corporation, New York, 1958. pp. 83–146.

3. Werner Jaeger, *Paideia: The Ideals of Greek Culture,* Oxford University Press, New York, 1945, Vol. i. p. 159.

4. Mintzberg, Henry, *The Nature of Managerial Work.* Harper & Row, New York, 1973. pp. 32–53.

5. Peter F. Drucker, *The Effective Executive.* Harper & Row, New York, 1967. p. 25.

6

Objectives

BE ALL THAT YOU CAN BE

On the wall of my living room there hangs a picture of a Bushi, a Japanese warrior-knight of the seventeenth century. It is a beautiful and valuable painting, but what attracted me most to that work of art was the expression on the warrior's face. The look in his eyes, the smile on his face, the dedication with which he was about to perform his duty—those qualities shone out across the centuries. That man enjoyed his work, found immense satisfaction in what he was trained to do, and was undoubtedly very good at his craft. Even his spirited white steed had a look of dedicated enjoyment in his eyes!

There is no greater satisfaction in life than that of fulfilling your potential—becoming what your heart and soul told you to become. That should be the first objective on your agenda. Since you have chosen the road of leadership, objectives will assume a great deal of significance to you. There are all kinds of objectives. In fact, one of the chief schools of management is called "Management by

Objectives" (MBO). It is important, however, that you consider managing *yourself* by objectives first before moving on to the wider scene of the organizational world. To begin with, the following anecdote may help to illustrate the point.

A traveler came across three men building a house. He stopped to ask the first man what he was doing. "Working very hard," the first man replied, perspiring. The traveler then asked the second man what he was doing. "I'm the best carpenter in the county, and I'm practicing my trade," the second man replied. He then asked the third man what he was doing. "Why, I'm building the most beautiful house in this area," he replied.

Each of the three men that the traveler questioned had a different objective in sight; only the third worker had any idea of the ultimate objective—a beautiful house. In one sense, building a beautiful house is your main objective also. The house will remain unseen, however, and you'll find that you'll not be able to appreciate it very much by yourself. But the greater the care and effort that went into building the house, the more it will be admired by others. The house that you cannot see will be the house of your reputation, and can become a structure that will attract the attention of those around you. The construction of your house will be made up of many different materials; yet, integrated into a symmetrical and well-coordinated whole, your house may well become the most beautiful and best constructed house in your neighborhood.

What are the materials that your house will be made up of? The first and perhaps most important material is *integrity*. That is a word which often causes confusion. It is sometimes used as a synonym for honesty. Even the dictionary has trouble with this widely used, yet dimly understood word. My *Webster's Dictionary* defines integrity as "unimpaired condition, adherence to a moral, artistic or other code, or the quality of being complete or undivided." This doesn't seem to help us very much, however, because there is confusion as to what the word integrity means to us. For Harry Levinson, in *The Exceptional Executive,*[1] integrity means what has become an accepted vernacular expression, "getting it all together." Levinson points out that integrity is composed of elements or qualities that can only be achieved by maturity. These are: intimate or close relationships with others, combat, leadership, love, inspiration, and the ability to share all these things with others by teaching them what you have learned.

The integrated man or woman, therefore, is the person who has achieved maturity because he or she has been able to engage in friendly rivalry with others, form intimate relationships that are meaningful, can exercise leadership with responsibility, and is willing to show others how they can achieve the same goals. If integrity is used as a synonym for honesty, it's not so much because the person of integrity is honest to the world; it's because the person of integrity is honest with *himself.* And all honesty begins with yourself. Dishonesty with oneself or with others destroys integrity because it strikes at the foundation of that beautiful house that we are building. Integrity means wholeness and unity. Conversely, dishonesty destroys the unity of truth, and will tear away the most important part of our house—integrity. Samuel Johnson said it well: "Integrity without knowledge is weak and useless, and knowledge without integrity is dangerous and dreadful."

As I have already suggested, integrity means that you can have relationships with others that only mature persons can accept and work with. One of these kinds of relationships means being able to engage others in friendly rivalry without feeling threatened. The old cliche that competition is healthy may be true, but it's only true of those who have enough maturity to be able to accept competition without coming unglued. Thus rivalry within your organization has to be accepted by you as a mature person. It means the avoidance of backbiting, manipulating others, and staying away from the "dirty-tricks" people. You are thus a whole person who is not intimidated by threats or attempts to manipulate you. You are also a person who is willing to share the fruits of your learning and experience with others. That is, you are willing to teach others what you know, and you are willing to assist them up the same ladder that you have already climbed yourself.

Integrity is a word that you will learn to value more as you get closer to the top leadership of your organization. You'll also see others looking your house over to see if it's made up of integrity, because only such a person can really ever be trusted to accomplish a task successfully. The principal characteristic of all great men and women has been integrity. Great leaders—political, industrial, managerial—have all been marked for their greatness because of their integrity. The integrated person is the exceptional person.

By now you are asking, "If integrity is so important, why haven't I heard more about it? How can I acquire it?" You haven't heard much about it as a quality of leadership because heretofore it has been assumed that integrity has been one of those ephemeral inherited traits that people either had or didn't have. "Phil's a great guy—what integrity!" might be an often-heard comment that indicated that Phil must possess some magical qualities. Conversely, saying that "Harry can't be trusted—he has no integrity," indicates that poor Harry was born without it, and that he'll never be able to acquire it. To those who believe this, they're in for a shock, because integrity is acquired, not inherited. It's a process like any other process of life that we go through and can learn if we are willing to use our intelligence and our wills. The basic steps towards acquiring integrity—and the reputation that goes with it—for yourself are:

1. In your relations with others, always strive to be friendly and consistent. Friendships are strong because they are built on consistency.
2. Never be rattled by competition. Jealousy and bitter rivalry have no real place in an organization, and

the person who depends on those traits is immature,
i.e. has no integrity.

3. Be always willing to share your knowledge and expertise with others. Never try to make a secret of your job or clothe it in mystery.

4. Dishonesty and exaggeration (an offshoot of dishonesty) have no place in the person of integrity.

5. A person with integrity is a person who is both consistent and reliable. Building a reputation for integrity means letting the world know by your actions and behavior that you possess the qualities of consistency and reliability.

The second important ingredient of your house will be *dedication.* Once again, if we turn to the dictionary for a definition, we see that *Webster's* defines dedication as "self-sacrificing devotion." It sounds like someone reading a citation for a Medal of Honor recipient. In another sense, however, it really is a requirement for those who lead. Indeed, dedication is the distinguishing mark of the executive who is fired up by his own enthusiasm, and can communicate that enthusiasm to those around him. Dedication also makes life worth living because it means striving for goals that are worth striving for. It means purposeful goal-oriented activity, the kind that is meant to serve the spirit and the kind of activity that gives you back much more in satisfaction, knowing that you have made an achievement far greater than any mere monetary or material reward could ever provide. Dedication also means commitment—the kind of commitment that will replace the apathy and indifference that mark the uncommitted. As John Gardner pointed out in his inspiring book, *Excellence:*

The best-kept secret in America today is that people would rather work hard for something they believe in than enjoy a pampered idleness.[2]

By this time, it is a poorly kept secret that the key to the industrial success of modern Japan has been the spirit of dedication which every worker, every executive, and every secretary in Japanese corporations have displayed over the years since World War II that has enabled them to capture such a sizable share of the world market.

Dedication is food for the spirit; it gives us something outside of ourselves to believe in, and moves us away from self-indulgence to external goals. It is a fitting complementary quality to that first ingredient of our house, integrity. People do not really want to live for themselves. That is one of the greatest secrets of human existence that you must learn if you are to become a truly dedicated leader. What life is really about, therefore, is achievement—external goals and the satisfaction that comes from striving for those goals. All great social and political movements have been marked by dedication; All great art; all great inventions; all great discoveries; and certainly all great leaders. It's what keeps the tough going when the going gets tough. As O. H. Ohmann points out in a thoughtful essay:

> Many great executives I have known have something deep inside that supports them; something they trust when the going gets tough; something ultimate; something personal; something beyond reason—in short a deep-rooted skyhook which brings them calm and confidence when they stand alone.[3]

That "something" is dedication, and it can be a very powerful force when used properly.

Of course, there is also dedication to the wrong cause; dedication without moral purpose; dedication to bad ends. So one must be careful that he is following a nondestructive path. Achieving the goals that we dedicate ourselves to can be a distressing experience. This simply proves that getting there is more than half the fun. The successful executive therefore is restless, moves from goal to goal, and is never really satisfied. His satisfaction comes from achieving new objectives all the time. And he can only achieve those objectives when he is *dedicated!* Remember, dedication comes from within. It does not come from your organization *to* you; instead it goes *from* you to those in your organization. It is your spirit of dedication that will arouse and enthuse those people whom you come in contact with in your organization that will make your sense of dedication a genuine asset to your house. That is what will make you a worthy leader.

The third ingredient of your house is *service.* It is the willingness to serve, to give of yourself as much as you can while seeking no reward that will mark you as a leader. "How can I be of service?" or "In what way can I contribute?" are often-heard expressions that best express this quality. The executive who is committed to this goal of service also sees his organization in a different light than others who think of their roles as simply fulfilling a function like accounting or engineering. This type of executive who is concerned about his contribution also is mindful of the contribution that his organization is making to society, to its customers, etc. In fact, I suspect rather strongly that every time an organization, and the people in it, concentrate on their function and forget about their overall responsibility, that organization is without purpose and spirit; and the people within it are afflicted with the same disease. Such organizations are not long for this world because their souls are dead; they really have no purpose, having lost it all in a miasmatic haze of pointless compartmentalization. Each person concerned with only his or her function and not worrying about the overall performance of the organization is a sure recipe for failure.

Instead of saying, "It's not my job ...," the person who wants to serve, says "How can I help?"; "What else can I do?" Such a person is really saying that he or she wants to do everything in their power to be of service, i.e. help to make the organization successful even if it's not in their job description. The executive who behaves in this fashion is setting a standard of sacrifice that will raise the standards and achievements of everyone around him. Focusing on the ideal of service keeps the executive mindful of the need for an integrated organization. In today's world of specialization, engineers are unable to communicate with accountants; chemists cannot relate to personnel managers, and so on. Yet, there is a tremendous need for just the kind of "specialist" who can break down the lines of separation and can get people to think in terms of their *total* contribution to the overall health of their organization, and ultimately, to society. The executive who leads by serving and contributing all that he or she can sets up a pattern of teamwork that is hard to beat. If all of the members of the organization thought in terms of their contribution to the general success of their company, each would realize that they were much more than mere cogs in the company wheel. The effective executive is the one who will try his best to promote that kind of spirit and service by constantly asking, "How can I serve better?" Thus, *service* as the third part of our house of reputation, if practiced and used, will mark you as a person of unusual zeal and one who is concerned about your organization's success *as* an organization. You are thus a whole person who worries about the whole organization.

The fourth part of your house of reputation is *discipline.* Without discipline, your house would collapse much like a house of cards. Discipline is what holds your house together, and it is a fourth quality that you must cultivate if you are to become an effective leader. Discipline and self-control are synonymous. These qualities are the mark of the inner-directed, free individual who knows what he is after, and knows how to organize his activities and behavior in the successful pursuit of those goals.

In a world such as we now live in, where 75 percent of mankind lives in a form of semislavery, self-discipline is what keeps us free. John Gardner points out that "The world is full of people who believe that men need masters."[4] Totalitarians control their populations by external force. A free people who believe in a system of free enterprise and the worth of the individual thrive on the notion that individual men and women can exercise enough responsibility and self-discipline to go after their own goals without being regulated by some taskmaster, set over them to impose the will of the state as a substitute for the will of the individual.

As a leader, the amount of discipline that you can exercise over yourself will have a great deal to do with reaching your goals. It is well recognized that discipline and morale go hand in hand. Only discipline can force you to keep striving and to practice constantly the virtues that your house is made up of.

As modern industry continues to enlarge and as government bureaucracy swells to even greater proportions, the need for discipline grows at a very rapid pace. The reason? The self-directed individual becomes an even greater necessity in an organizational world where autonomy and self-direction are increasingly the rule. One of the best examples of this kind of need comes from the communist world. At the beginning, communist governments felt that they could not trust their managers to make decisions on their own. Instead, they formed centralized hierarchies, ruled by the guardians of the Communist Party, who made all the decisions for the managers who were no better than a bunch of automatons. But a dysfunctional disease began to emerge in these societies. It was the disease of uncertainty and dependence, and it meant that managers in these societies were frozen into inaction, constantly waiting to be told what to do next by the hierarchy above them. The results in most of these societies was a much slower rate of growth, and an inability to innovate. What should have been eager, zealous, innovative managers were thus transformed into a generation of bungling bureaucrats, and the societies that they were supposed to serve suffered needlessly.

Communist societies have come to terms with this problem in recent years, and have recognized the need to encourage managers to use their initiative and self-discipline. The results have been encouraging, and have proven that the inner-directed manager who has discipline and motivation can create his objectives and strive to reach them without constant prodding from above.

What has happened in communist societies stands as proof that the manager who knows what his objectives are, and is willing to make sacrifices to reach those objectives, will perform in a much better way than the manager who has to be constantly threatened. The inner-directed, autonomous manager was once again proven to be much more successful.

Discipline is what will make it possible for you to be able to use those other qualities—integrity, dedication, and service—in a way that will make you a truly great leader.

Our first rule, then, is: *Your first objective is to build the house of your reputation. It contains integrity, dedication, and service and is held together by discipline.*

THE BIGGEST JOB OF ALL

Your responsibilities as a manager will stretch over more territory than anyone else's in your organization. A second set of objectives, therefore, is to consider what the goals of good management—the biggest job of all—consist of.

When management science first appeared on the scene sometime around the turn of the century, it was thought that the manager's job was composed of five basic functions, namely, planning, organizing, coordinating, commanding, and controlling. Henri Fayol devised this system in 1916. Later, more functions were added, such as staffing, reporting, and budgeting. Thus the acronym, POSDCORB,[5] was ultimately derived in the early 30s while management science was still in its infancy. But the POSDCORB formula only described a variety of *functions* that the manager was supposed to perform. It never really described in any integrated fashion precisely what a manager's overall contribution to the success of his organization should consist of. In other words, the manager was simply sliced up in several different ways, each part of him being responsible for one of the functions. Such a view was found to have been shortsighted and disintegrative, to say the least.

Today's view of managerial work is quite different. Unlike the earlier, more formal schools of management, where everyone had his place and where there was a place for everyone, modern management science is more geared to rapid change and anticipatory developments. Managers, similarly, are expected to be as adaptive and flexible as possible. That is why the idea of *Management by Objectives* has become so popular. This school of thought encourages participatory management, and has spread the responsibility for achieving the goals (objectives) of the organization over a wide variety of people. Indeed, under this scheme, all of the personnel within an organization can be asked to participate by establishing the objectives that they hope to accomplish during the next month or the next 6 months. Thus, while the manager's job has become more diversified and more integrative, it has also become much more varied, and the manager of today finds himself much more preoccupied with the ultimate goals of his organization than the manager of yesteryear. Let us next consider what these new tasks of management are, and why they are more integrative than the older formulas that dealt more with specific functions.

There are three general categories that best define the objectives-setting roles of managers. In each category, there are also a number of subcategories. These categories are listed in Table 6–1.

The first general category, that of decision maker, is illustrated by the accompanying Figure 6–1. The manager makes the decisions that are central to the survival of his organization. The scope of his decision making depends to a great extent, of course, on the size of his organization, the scope of the manager's job, and the problem at hand. Let's now take a look at Figure 6–1 and attempt to follow each step in the decision-making steps that will lead to the ultimate objective—survival.

The organization's survival needs give rise to a number of problems to be solved. Let's say that our manager is the product manager of a medium-size firm. The present sales volume has remained stationary over the past year. The firm needs to increase its sales volume, and the product

Table 6–1
Objectives-Setting Roles of Managers.

Chief Roles	Decision Maker	Guardian	Teacher
Subcategories	Planning	Negotiator	Motivator
	Allocating	Monitor	Exemplifier
	Prioritizing	Liaison	Mentor
	Entrepreneur	Crisis Manager	
	Strategist		

manager has an important question to be resolved. Should the firm come out with a new line of products or should it try to upgrade the old ones? This is essentially the question being posed to the product manager in Phase I of Figure 6–1.

Phase II shows the manager considering two plans. Plan 1 is the plan for developing a new line of products. Plan 2 is taking some kind of action to increase sales of the present line of products (perhaps new packaging?). At the Phase-II level, there are both external and internal environmental factors to be considered. External factors might include the climate of the marketplace or of the economy in general; or perhaps the attitude of the present customers towards the product (customer acceptance). There are also internal factors such as the amount of capital available for new product development or the number of people available to do research for a new product, etc. At the Phase-III level, both plans 1 and 2 are considered quite operative and the manager has both options wide open to him. However, while plans 1 and 2 are under active consideration, environmental factors could be shifting. Government regulations might force a change in the design of his product for example, or the budget available for new development may have shrunk suddenly. Thus, there are always pressures and influences from the environment that will play a role in the manager's decisions.

Phase IV represents a further refinement in the potential plans by the manager. Plan 1a would represent an

How Managers Make Decisions

External environment

Internal environment

Feedback

| Phase I | Phase II | Phase III | Phase IV | Phase V | Phase VI |

Survival needs

Problems to be solved

Manager

Plan 1

Plan 2

Plan 1a

Plan 1b

Plan 2a

Plan 2b

Decision

Implementation

all-out campaign that would develop an entirely new product, and would be the most expensive of all. Plan 1b would represent a new product development, but with a smaller budget. Plan 2a would represent an expanded advertising campaign to push the old product, while Plan 2b would represent a much more conservative approach. At the same time that the manager is studying changing market trends, he is conferring with his staff and is exchanging ideas with both his superiors and his opposite numbers in other departments of his organization.

Phase V shows the final development of the various plans, including such things as cost estimates, market factors, feasibility studies, etc.

Phase VI represents the final decision and the resulting implementation of the plan. Feedback from the implementation not only affects the survival needs of the organization, but will also affect the future decisions of the manager. Throughout the entire process, the manager has had to stay on top of many factors. At every single phase of the development of objectives, there have been interruptions and new environmental changes that the manager has constantly had to keep in mind. From beginning to end, the decision-making process is under constant bombardment by new, and sometimes, startling changes. Therefore, the planning activities of the manager are a dynamic, not a static, process. Because there is constant flux (change), the process never really slows down, and there is the constant need for readjustment to new conditions. In fact, by the time the manager reaches his or her final decision, market conditions might have changed radically, so that even the final decision might find itself subjected to new demands. The result? The manager must keep on his toes, and must be constantly aware of new conditions and new changes. He or she must be continually allowing for input at any place along the feedback line that will affect both the immediate and long-range determination of objectives.

In addition to the decision-making responsibilities that the manager has, the subordinate roles that are played by the manager are also quite important, as they are all a part of that same decision-making process. As a *planner,* the manager must mesh with the survival needs (objectives) of the organization. This means setting up a plan that has definite specifics, timetables, etc. As an *allocator,* the manager has to see to it that enough resources (personnel, material, money) will be available at the right times and in the right places so that the plan can be accomplished. The manager must also be a *prioritizer.* That is, he or she must establish the priorities for the plan. Perhaps, as in our example above, the demand and need for new products is extremely important. The manager's job, then, will be to establish that as a priority objective, and to set up a series of categories that will clearly demonstrate a priority for each one. Thus, a new product might have a class I priority; while pushing sales of the older products might have a class IV priority.

The manager must also act as an entrepreneur in many cases. That is, he or she must be imaginative, innovative, and somewhat daring. This would be especially true of a product manager, as in our example. Being an entrepreneur means having the desire and the ability to take risks. Finally, as a decision maker, the manager is also a strategist. The ability to determine the ultimate outcome of the decisions now being made is the stuff of which crystal ball wizardry is made. Yet, it is a necessary quality of good managerial decision making. Shrewd guessing is partly the result of intuition, of experience, and of education. Good strategy is the result of plotting a number of possible outcomes against the number of alternatives open to you. There can be no exact determination of the outcome of your decision; but you cannot be faulted if you have taken every possible factor into account *before* making your decision: after your decision it is too late.

The second category of objectives are those that include the role of *guardian.* As a guardian, the manager must oversee the maintenance problems of his organization. Strategy is simply not enough because you cannot sit alone and plan strategy unless you know that there will be enough troops (competent, qualified, satisfied people) or a reasonably smooth running organization on which you can base your strategic decisions. Keeping your organization running on an even keel is as important a part of your job as planning for long-range strategy. The guardian's tasks are those of negotiator, monitor, liaison, and crisis manager. As *negotiator,* the manager may have to deal with union problems or may have to carry on negotiations with other departments or with outside agencies, such as the federal government. Negotiating skills are different from those required normally of a manager because the negotiator is frequently on the defensive. He is seeking compromise, and is usually willing to make concessions. In these days of consumer interest groups and a much more demanding public, the negotiating skills of managers are in much higher demand than ever before. Even large corporations, such as General Motors, find themselves having to use the skills of negotiators in dealing with Congress, labor unions, or the Environmental Protection Agency, to name but a few. Negotiating essentially means, therefore, bargaining. Giving concessions, but getting them as well; and the successful executive is one who can negotiate so that his organization can continue to navigate.

As a *monitor,* the successful executive trains himself to keep tuned to his organization and to constantly measure the successes and failures of his group. This is quite analogous to listening to your car engine while it is running, and maintaining a watchful eye on the gauges. Monitoring is essentially trouble-shooting. It is looking for problems, and trying to keep them from disrupting the organization before it gets to the crisis stage.

As a *liaison,* the manager makes it his or her business to serve as a link between his department and other departments, not only to receive input but to send forth information to other segments as well. Without proper liaison activity, there can be no transmission of intelligence, and intelligent action has to be based on informed, cooperative linkage. The manager acting as liaison is an important link in that chain.

As a *manager of crisis,* the executive has to be constantly ready for crisis. This means developing contingency plans and maintaining a good monitoring schedule. The manager's role as a guardian certainly must include the necessity of dealing with crisis whenever it arises. A crisis that is poorly handled can quickly turn into a disaster.

Perhaps the most important role that the manager has is that of a *teacher.* He must pass on to others the knowledge and expertise that he or she has acquired over the years. Ask any successful man or woman who had the greatest influence over their lives, and the answer will invariably describe someone who has taught them. It could be a parent, a boss, a colleague, or a "teacher," but in any case, it was a person who showed them how to be successful. As every successful person has his or her mentor, so do successful people assume responsibility for guiding those who are under their tutelage. Their styles may be different, but the end results are the same. They have urged, inspired, and enthused those around them, while giving unselfishly of their experiences and accumulated wisdom. More importantly, the one who teaches is also the model for his or her proteges. Even as we imitate our parents when we are children, so we emulate those who guide our lives when we are older. In fact, sometimes such emulation amounts to something akin to hero worship, and a great difficulty arises in regarding the object of worship as a superhuman being with special powers. Such thinking is dangerous, and those who are in this special position should always remind their followers that they are human as well. I once studied under a philosopher whose name is known the world over. I regarded him with great awe. One day after my summer vacation, this great and revered man asked me how my summer vacation was. I answered by recounting my financial difficulties, my research difficulties, etc. I then asked him how *his* summer was. I expected him to tell me about his latest book or his latest travels. Instead he said, "Oh, I've also had a difficult summer. My car broke down. The furnance had to be fixed, and it was all very expensive!" Then and there, I realized that even this great man was a human being just like me, and was not to be blindly worshiped.

We should consider ourselves extremely fortunate if we have the opportunity to learn from a highly regarded or successful person. Such individuals are rare, and if they are unselfish and kind enough to share their wisdom with you, then be sure to drink as deeply as you can at their well.

Those executives who think of themselves properly as teachers would undoubtedly agree that they have the responsibility of motivating the people around them. Urging people on is not always easy. Frequently the rewards are not always there, and people cannot achieve much joy or satisfaction from doing their jobs more successfully. But it is the job of the leader as teacher to convince them that what they are doing *is* worthwhile. If you are that leader and if you are a role model, your task in this respect will be a lot easier because the people under you will want to emulate you in order to acquire your approval. But you must be the kind of boss who inspires people to seek your approval. A kind word or a pat on the back from someone who is not respected is *not* the same as from someone who is looked up to as a role model.

It used to be part of officers' training in the United States Marine Corps that no officer should ask any of his men to do anything that he himself was not capable of or willing to do. The same should be said of executive leadership. The executive as a teacher is also an *exemplifier.* He is telling his subordinates not to do as he says, but to do as he does. Setting an example for those around you, therefore, must be seen as an important part of your job as a teacher.

Finally, the executive who is a good teacher is also a *mentor.* The dictionary defines mentor as one who is a wise and valued counselor. As a teacher of others, it may one day become your great fortune to become the mentor of someone who will reflect great credit on you. The good mentor guides and carefully points out the road ahead to those under his care. Obviously, being a mentor involves much more than just teaching someone a skill. Thomas Edison was a great mentor. His laboratory at Menlo Park was a training ground for some of the greatest inventors and scientists of the twentieth century. Similarly, Alfred Sloan, one of the founders of General Motors, was also a great mentor. Sloan's main goals were to develop the talents of those around him. That was the only real way to build a truly great organization. And to do that you had to take young people under your wing; you had to become someone's mentor; you had to become responsible in a way for their success or failure in life. The late Dwight D. Eisenhower once wrote about his mentor, General Fox Connor:

> Life with General Connor was a sort of graduate school in military affairs and the humanities, leavened by a man who was experienced in his knowledge of men and their conduct. I can never adequately express my gratitude to this one gentleman.[6]

Being someone's mentor is a great responsibility; but it's also a great privilege.

The executive is a teacher because he or she has also been a student. Our second rule, then, is: *The manager's job encompasses the roles of decision maker, guardian, and teacher. No manager can succeed who fails to keep these roles constantly in mind.*

How the Object Becomes the Subject

Ever since social organization first appeared on this planet, Management by Objectives has been a basic tool of human culture. Certainly the ancient Egyptians used it to build their colossal pyramids. The Romans could not have built their far-flung, vast empire without sound administration and a clear idea of what they wanted to do. What was true of the ancients rapidly became true of corporate society (both private and public) in the twentieth century. Management science quickly found the tools with which to achieve their goals.

Management by Objectives is an art as well as a science, and it is an art that you should become well versed in because it will be a tremendous asset in your career as a manager.

First, what is Management by Objectives? We could begin by offering a couple of definitions from two authors who have had a great deal to do with putting it into practice. The first author, Peter Drucker, has sometimes been described as the man who invented the system of Management by Objectives. At any rate, he has had a great deal to do with conceptualizing the methodology of modern organizations. In his book, *Management: Tasks, Responsibilities, Practices,* he writes:

> Management by objectives and self-control may properly be called a philosophy of management. It rests on a concept of the job of management . . . rests on a concept of human action, behavior, and motivation.[7]

Another definition that is perhaps more specific is offered by Karl Albrecht:

> Management by Objectives is nothing more—nor less—than an observable *pattern of behavior* on the part of a manager, characterized by studying the anticipated future, determining what payoff conditions to bring about for that anticipated future, and guiding the efforts of the people of the organization so that they accomplish these objectives while deriving personal and individual benefits in doing so.[8]

There appear to be as many different definitions of Management by Objectives as there are writers on the subject. Herewith is my own:

> Management by Objectives is the art of focusing all of the resources available on the attainment of specific goals within

a specific period of time. Management by Objectives must therefore include measurable goals, measurable results, and some means of external guidance towards the achievement of those goals.

Management by Objectives is a means of achieving goals. Nothing more, nothing less, Whether your goals are to satisfy as many public welfare clients as possible or to become the biggest corporate giant in history, Management by Objectives can be successfully utilized in the pursuit of those goals. Albrecht is correct when he points out that there must be some kind of payoff as a part of the end process of any Management by Objectives. Any system of reward that can demonstrate that the goals have been satisfactorily achieved can be defined as a "payoff."

There are a number of steps that can serve as a guide to the techniques of MBO. They are:

1. The general objectives of the organization must first be outlined. These include the goals, the purpose, and the direction that the organization wishes to pursue.

2. The general objectives are then refined into their specific components, i.e. from "we must increase sales" to "we must increase sales by $100,000 within the next fiscal year."

3. Each department manager must then be asked to define his or her objectives within the stated goals of the organization. The questions, When? Where? Why? How? should be answered as specifically as possible.

4. All of the objectives as well as all of the *specific* means of achieving those objectives should be committed to paper. Each person in the organization who has drawn up a set of objectives must commit himself to their achievement.

5. At the end of the specified period of time, it then becomes management's task to measure the levels of achievement of goals. Suitable rewards based on achievement can be a part of the process.

Management by Objectives should be a process that involves as many people in the organization as possible. It is the kind of technique that allows the general goals of the organization to filter down to the lowest level. Such goals (to survive, to satisfy our clients, to become the biggest or the best) then can become an intrinsic part of the spirit of all of the personnel, from the president to the maintenance crew. Just as no person can survive for long without meaningful goals in his or her life, neither can an organization survive for very long if it cannot develop goals and goal-oriented methods for achieving them. The most important point to remember is that MBO will not work unless the goals it establishes are measurable ones. Bearing in mind that Management by Objectives must be as concrete and as measurable as possible, let's look at an example of how a mythical organization, the NRG Corporation might use MBO at different levels:

NRG Corporation

Office of the president
General objectives of the corporation:

Measure?

1. Increase sales by 15 percent for the next fiscal year.
2. Expand the number of regional sales managers by 5 percent.
3. Increase production efficiency.
4. Find a better and cheaper source of raw materials.

Vice president in charge of sales
Objectives:

Measure?

1. Increase sales by 15 percent.
2. Develop new sales and advertising techniques.
3. Spend more time in the field.
4. Analyze sources of customer resistance to product.
5. Spend more time with sales managers.

Sales manager
   Objectives:

Measure?
{
1. Spend more time with salesmen.
2. Trouble-shoot dissatisfied customers.
3. Increase salesman's more efficient use of time.
4. Develop a better reporting system for salesmen.
}

Salesman
   Objectives:

Measure?
{
1. Increase number of calls.
2. Study presentation techniques more.
3. Consult more with sales manager.
4. Analyze sales presentations that fizzled. Discuss them with sales manager.
}

The above example only deals with one category of the overall objectives of the NRG Corporation. If we wanted to, we could describe every segment (i.e. production, shipping, procurement) of the corporation as a study in the achievement of objectives. At every level, the question "Measure?" comes up because each level of effort must include criteria that are measurable. That is the only way to learn whether or not progress has been made. It is also the only way to provide suitable rewards for achievement. Also, it is important to note that from the president of NRG on down to the salesman in the field, each person or department is involved in establishing their own set of objectives and their own criteria. They are, of course, consonant with the overall objectives of the president (sell more products, have more satisfied customers). Moreover, each department must answer the questions, "WHEN?, WHERE?, WHY?, HOW?" in as detailed a fashion as possible. Thus, each level of the NRG Corporation has become a part of the entire process of setting objectives. As a result, each level and each person involved in that process is also accountable for the success or failure of those objectives. In the entire process, no one twisted anyone else's arm. Each was asked what he could do to enhance the success of the corporation, and each responded with his or her set of objectives. Thus, MBO is a procedure that places heavy reliance on the individual and the contribution that he or she can make to the ultimate success of the organization. It is a far cry from the authoritarian and highly centralized systems of yesteryear. Those systems failed because they were unimaginative and thought that only the carrot-and-stick techniques used on jackasses would work. They forgot that the jackass can have a will and mind of his own, and be a pretty stubborn critter to boot!

Finally, it is important to remember that MBO is a tool, not a goal in itself. If it is used as a tool, it can be tremendously helpful, but if we make a fetish of it, and use the *process* of MBO as a goal rather than a means, we shall have defeated our purpose altogether. That is the greatest danger that MBO poses—the danger of misuse. Our third rule, then, is: *Management by Objectives is an effective means for improving the performance of an organization, but it must be used only as a means, not as an end.*

As we have seen, there are all kinds of objectives—personal, social, corporate. As a rising leader in the organizational world, it will benefit you greatly to take the establishment of goals seriously, for that is the only way that you are going to be able to progress.

Summary

There are four qualities that should become part of your personal objectives. They are acquired through effort and concentration, and are *not* inherited. The four qualities are integrity, dedication, service, and discipline. Integrity represents the person who is integrated, whole, and can relate to the rest of the world in a mature way. Dedication means devotion or loyalty; service means sacrifice; and discipline means constant attention to goals and not becoming easily sidetracked.

Managers have a number of different functions including decision making, guardianship, and teaching. Each of these general functions is crucial to the managerial role, and no organization can be complete without them. The planning function is especially important, and it must be seen as a dynamic, not a static process. The guardian function is similarly important because the organization has to be maintained—cared for and fed—even while all of the other processes are ongoing. The teaching function of the executive provides the means for sharing the accumulated wisdom and knowledge of the executive that will result in the long-range propagation of the organization's goals and successes.

Finally, the art and science of Management by Objectives (MBO) must be seriously considered as a tool of good management because it enables us to set and work toward goals. We are also able to do this in such a manner as to involve personnel at all levels of the organization in its objectives. This will give them a sense of participation as well as accountability.

THE THREE RULES OF SETTING OBJECTIVES

1. Your first objective is to build the house of your reputation. It contains integrity, dedication, and service, and is held together by discipline
2. The manager's job encompasses the roles of decision maker, guardian, and teacher. No manager can succeed who fails to keep these roles constantly in mind.
3. Management by Objectives is an effective means for improving the performance of an organization, but it must be used only as a means, not as an end.

EXERCISES FOR CHAPTER 6

1. Observe a manager at work. Keep track of the way in which he spends his day. Which of his roles seem most important? Which seem least important? There are many

organizations whose executives would welcome you as a "1-day intern," if you explain that this is an educational project. This could be a public agency, a private nonprofit agency, or a private organization.

2. Develop your skill at negotiation. Draw up a simulation and with one or two friends, engage in a role-playing situation. Two parties can do the negotiating; a third party can be the arbitrator and make the awards. Example: The workers at your plant have declared a wildcat strike. The issue? A union member has been fired by your foreman because of shoddy work. The worker complains that he was reassigned to this new job from which he was subsequently fired, and that he did excellent work at his old job. The foreman agrees that he was a good worker, but that his old job has now become obsolete. The wildcat strike is in violation of a previous contract between your company and the workers' union. Now, the union is also making a list of demands before they will agree to go back to work. Most of these demands have nothing to do with the fired worker. Your simulation should include a list of worker demands, and a list of counter demands by you. See how many you can draw up, and see how skillfully you can negotiate. Let the arbitrator be the judge and make the final award.

3. Make a list of the personal objectives that you see as goals for yourself. Develop a timetable and a methodology for acquiring these goals. How will you measure your achievements?

NOTES

1. Harry Levinson, *The Exceptional Executive.* Mentor, New York, 1971, p. 251–252.

2. John W. Gardner, *Excellence.* Harper & Bros., New York, 1961. p. 148.

3. O. H. Ohmann, "Skyhooks," in *Harvard Business Review on Management,* Harper & Row, New York, 1975. p. 702.

4. Gardner, op. cit., p. 147.

5. Planning, organizing, staffing, directing, coordinating, reporting, and budgeting.

6. Dwight D. Eisenhower, *At Ease: Stories I Tell to Friends,* Doubleday, New York, 1967, p. 136.

7. Peter F. Drucker, *Management: Tasks, Responsibilities, Practices,* Harper & Row, New York, 1973, p. 442.

8. Karl Albrecht, *Successful Management by Objectives,* Prentice-Hall, Englewood Cliffs, N.J., 1978, p. 20.

7
We

$\mathcal{U}$nless you go into business for yourself, you'll probably end up as an executive in some kind of organization.
Therefore, it is important to acquire an understanding of
how and why organizations function, their natures, characteristics, and diversity. Organizational behavior has
become an intensive study of management specialists in
the past few years, and we can learn much from these
studies. For your own successful future, you've got to know
the territory; moreover, a better acquaintance with the
sizes and kinds of organizations that exist today will be a
great asset in helping you make your career choice more
wisely.

TELLING THE TREES FROM THE FOREST

Organizations are like people—they come in all shapes
and sizes. They have unique personalities, and they suffer
from internal conflict. Moreover, they are constantly adjusting to new conditions. As there are so many different

varieties it will pay for us to look at some of them, and understand what differences exist between private and public sector organizations, for example; or between large and small organizations; or between highly structured and loosely structured organizations.

The first major kinds of organizations to look at are those in the public sector. The proliferation of government agencies over the past decade is bewildering. There are now 12 Cabinet-level agencies, and a 13th at this writing appears imminent (Department of Education). A recent report indicates that the number of federal employees is at the highest level in history. The economic and energy crises have caused citizens to demand more services than ever before from government at all three levels—federal, state, and local; and the public's thirst for more government does not yet appear to be on the verge of declining. Even private-sector corporations have been reluctant to see the hand of government removed from their midst. When it was proposed that the trucking industry be deregulated during the energy crisis of 1979, for example, a howl of protest went up from the industry, and predictions of chaos and turmoil were being made if the industry no longer came under the watchful eye of the Interstate Commerce Commission. While the relationship between private industry and government in the United States can hardly be described as a "honeymoon," private industry has come to find that government can be at least as helpful as it has been perceived to be hurtful. During your career, you will come into contact with the government in at least one of two ways. First, you will have to deal with the bureaucracy; second, you may find yourself employed by one of the many agencies of government. Indeed, government agencies recruit their executives from the private sector of both the corporate and the academic worlds. It is a well-known fact of government life that many executives work for an average of 5 years for a government agency, and then transfer to a private corporation. Some alternate between government and private industry, emulating the legendary $1-a-year executives who loaned themselves to government service during World War II. Most government executives who have joined the government from private industry usually have done so for a change of pace (perhaps as a reward for participating in an election campaign). These executives usually do not stay for longer than 5 years because of low salaries or red tape that they cannot cope with. The reasons for this can be best explained by analyzing some of the idiosyncracies of government.

Government agencies exist because they are mandated by Legislatures. It is these same bodies that give life and meaning to agencies, and those who give life can also take it away. That is a fact that is never lost on public servants. Indeed, in recent years, Legislatures have been intent on enacting "Sunset Laws" that could force the review of the value of an agency every few years and recommend the dissolution of agencies considered ineffective or expendable.

Government agencies have been granted both a monopoly in their area of concern as well as the police power over that jurisdiction. No one can go into competition with the Internal Revenue Service or the F.B.I., or the many thousands of other kinds of government agencies all over the country. Furthermore, they require compliance from everyone. Their power can be awesome. It follows from the monopolistic powers that government agencies have that their economic power is awesome as well. By a mere stroke of the pen, a government official can drastically alter market conditions and is undoubtedly in a good position to do favors for people. As an executive in either sector —public or private—you will undoubtedly find yourself in a position to either manipulate others by bribery or to be manipulated by the same tactics. My advice to you is— *don't!* It's not worth the price you'll have to pay.

Third, unlike private industry, government agencies have no voluntary market to respond to. Their services are offered on a "take it or leave it" basis, usually with heavy emphasis on "you'd better take it." Because government services are not offered for sale on a voluntary basis and because there is no competition, the chief complaint that most business executives have about government is that they have a "Manana Complex." While some of this criticism is true, there are competent and conscientious government executives who do take pride in their work. Businesses have customers whom they hope to satisfy; government agencies have constituents, and while there is no particular compulsion or need to satisfy them, a thoughtful bureaucrat will recognize that satisfied constituents are an excellent way of improving the relationship between his agency and the Legislature which provides the funds (budget) that support his agency.

The fourth point, which follows from the third, is that government agencies are not money makers, only money spenders. They exist solely on budget allocations from the legislative and executive branches. The principal way in which they improve their standing is by lobbying for a larger share of the budget. One point to bear in mind is that agencies do not necessarily *earn* an increased budget by performing better or by receiving public accolades. On the contrary, agencies must usually find another means of justifying their budgets, and these means usually consist of lobbying or of "playing ball" with certain legislators. In this way, many public agencies have become involved in playing the patronage game. Certainly, for the foreseeable future, government bureaucrats will never find a truly rational system for financing their agencies. If your career takes you down the road to a position in the public bureaucracy, the foregoing should be of some help to you in making you aware of the pitfalls of government service.

It is worthwhile considering a career in the government for yourself, for many reasons. As suggested earlier, there is a growing need for more government. It can be argued that that's not what the politicians say, but remember they're trying to get elected on a "put the government on a diet" platform. Watch what happens as soon as they are elected! At any rate, such problems as the American nation is now going to be confronted with, at least on a semi-permanent basis, are going to demand a larger and more entrenched bureaucracy than ever before. No matter how opposed people are to big government, new crises will cause the demand for more government. As a career option for yourself, therefore, it's worthwhile to consider government service, even if only for a short period. Those executives who have had at least some experiences in government will be in increasing demand by the private sector, because former government executives know their way around Washington better than private-sector people. Indeed, one of the complaints made over the years by columnists and activist groups has been that retired Pentagon generals join large, private defense contractors who will pay any price to get the expertise and "who you know" ability of the generals. Although employees of federal regulatory agencies are prohibited from coming from the industries that their agencies regulate, there is no law that prevents them from joining those industries once they have terminated their government connection. Washington, in fact, is awash with people who have formerly worked in government, and then have joined private organizations as highly paid lobbyists (perfectly legal). In the bureaucratic jungle, the person who can place a phone call to exactly the right government official can be worth his weight in gold! Over the next two or three decades at least, government is going to grow, not shrink, and a career of at least a few years as a federal or state executive can become very fruitful. I have known several people who have followed exactly the same kind of path that I just described, and they have all been extremely successful. So put a government career in your bag of options. To make government service even more attractive to executives, President Jimmy Carter established the Senior Executive Service under the Federal Civil Service Reform Act of 1977. A recent article describes some of the exciting changes that make a government career an exciting prospect:

The Senior Executive Service (SES)—the cornerstone of President Carter's plan for civil service reform—was officially implemented July 13, with the voluntary entry of 8,000 U.S. officials to the rank of "senior executive."

Members of the new SES have been promised substantial pay increases. . .amounting to as much as 20% of their salary.[1]

A second type of organization is the corporation, which is the rock upon which the free enterprise system is founded. The corporation as a form of organization was first given its rights as a legal person by the Supreme Court of The United States in 1886 (*Santa Clara County v. The Southern Pacific Railway*). At that time the court decided that corporations were entitled to the same protection as any other person under the Fifth and Fourteenth amendments of the Constitution. This situation remains unchanged to the present day, and the corporation has become the most popular national vehicle for conducting business that the country has ever known.

What is a corporation? Basically, it is an organization that is financed by the shareholders, who elect a board of directors (most of them are shareholders as well). The board of directors, in turn, hires and fires the managerial personnel, who, hopefully, will return a profit (dividends) to the shareholders, and everyone will go home happy, their pockets jingling with their newly found wealth. Corporations make money through entrepreneurial activity, by providing goods or services that will satisfy a demand in the market place. Perhaps they can create consumer demand as well by producing innovative new fashions and new products. Some corporations (public utilities, for example) have a monopoly on a product or a service; others may control the market by manipulation or price fixing, if they are large enough (that's when the Anti-Trust Division of the Department of Justice is supposed to step in). Most corporations, however, exist in a climate of competition with other similar businesses. These days, there is growing international competition as well. The American steel industry at this writing, for example, is quite worried about foreign competition, and many steel workers have lost their jobs.

In recent years, corporations have undergone many changes in their structures and methods of operation.

First, many of them have attempted to diversify which gives rise to the conglomerate. One large oil corporation has gone into the movie-making and publishing businesses, for example, while another has expanded from the liquor business to become one of the nations's largest fast-food franchisers. Still others have opened foreign plants or branches, and many foreign corporations have done the same in other countries, including the United States.

Another development in corporate structure has been the development of the multinational corporation. It has been described as a many-headed monster, all of the heads being connected to the same body, but each head doing business in different countries. Thus, the multinational corporation is not really subject to the laws of any one country; it is a law unto itself. Only the branches in particular countries are subject to the laws of those countries, but the body of that monster is able to make policy independent of any nation's laws or policies.

At the domestic level at least, corporations have found themselves having to respond increasingly to such new facts of life as government regulation, consumer interest groups, and rapidly changing national policies. More will be said about that later.

As I have already suggested, no two organizations are exactly alike. The same holds true for the corporation. Each has its own personality, quirks, and ambience. Whether it will be your first job or a career change, therefore, it is a good idea for you to exercise some caution in choosing an organization with the right "personality" for you. It can be an important career decision.

The third type of organization has a longer history than corporations. It is called the public service institution, and it originated in the First Amendment to the Constitution, i.e. "Congress shall make no law respecting an establishment of religion," which gave rise to a host of universities, hospitals, foundations, and other religious and charitable trusts. These are all operated under the nonprofit sections of the Internal Revenue Code, and are tax exempt.

The public service organization fills in many gray areas that are not serviced by either the corporation or the government agency. It fills in much-needed services such as hospitals and universities, and contracts with the general public as well as with corporations and government for the provision of services; but it does not exist to make a profit or capture a share of the marketplace. Indeed, it has been criticized by many writers on the subject as providing too much overkill in our society (too many hospitals and universities, for example). It has also been criticized as operating too inefficiently; hence the high cost of hospital services. Nevertheless, public service institutions are an integrally important part of society, and are funded by it, one way or another (through tax-exempt donations, for example).

How are public service institutions organized? Usually, they are chartered in the states in which they operate, and are organized by a self-perpetuating board of trustees or directors, who make the general policies, and then hire (or fire) the managerial personnel necessary to run the institution and carry out their policies. Sometimes, of course, the managers that they hire can convince the board of trustees to change or alter their policy direction, or sometimes the managerial personnel are really the ones who make policy altogether. At any rate, the managers of public service institutions are not entrepreneurs in the strict sense of the word. They might innovate, and they may develop plans to expand their areas of operations, etc., but it is not their chief function to return any profit to the directors. Instead, whatever monies are earned are turned back to the trustees and become part of the general fund from which a budget is developed for the institution.

Almost all nonprofit institutions operate in the fashion described above. Although a visiting stranger might conclude that they really do operate on a profit, such is not the case. Except for a few miscreants who have taken advantage of the tax laws, most of them really do operate on a nonprofit basis. And since there are limits to the money that they can earn and the number of areas in which they can diversify (many are restricted to certain functions by their charters), they can easily fall behind economically. Hence, there is a growing need for competent management for the public service institution. As Peter Drucker points out:

> Service institutions are an increasingly important part of our society. Schools and universities; research laboratories . . . all these are as much "institutions" as is the business firm, and, therefore are equally in need of management. They all have people who are designated to exercise the management function and who are paid for doing the management job—even though they may not be called "managers", but "administrators", "directors" or some other such title.[2]

Drucker goes on to point out that the public service institutions are the real growth sector of modern society, and he is quite right. These institutions are also extremely important to the survival of a nation made up of free institutions and priding itself on its individualism. They avoid the necessity of having an even larger government bureaucracy take over every nonbusiness function in our society. A career as a hospital administrator, for example, should be another option for you, as good managers in the public service will be increasing in demand. Our first rule, then, is: *In considering your career options, you should be well-acquainted with the three types of organizations that you could become affiliated with: government agencies, private corporations, and public service institutions. Each has its own peculiar structure and legal basis for existence.*

Old Wine in New Bottles

As I have already suggested, organizations are as old as mankind. But ancient man never was involved in organizations that were as complex as those of today. The industrial, technological, and computer revolutions that we have already witnessed have changed all that. Yet, there is a similarity insofar as man still depends on the organization for the accomplishment of his major tasks. Indeed, it can be argued that although organizations have become highly complex, they are still organizations after all, and we should not be fooled just by a new suit of clothes. Organizational structure, behavior, and function still exist as concepts, but their methods have changed; and the organization of yesteryear has had to respond to new challenges, hence "the old grey mare ain't what she used to be," as an old song suggests. Nevertheless, the general definition of what an organization is still remains valid: An organization is a group of people who cooperate for the achievement of defined goals. In effect, an organization is a living organism that responds to internal and external change and is constantly adjusting to new demands. Organizations go through a maturation process that includes the stages of youth, middle age, and old age, thus giving rise to the idea that the organization as a product of human endeavor is no better or worse than the people who control it. There are a number of concepts about organizational structure and behavior that we should be well-acquainted with. Let's take a look at them, each in turn.

Centralized Versus Decentralized Control

The question of the amount and quality of control that is to be exercised by the manager depends on a number of factors: the size and complexity of the organization, the amount of specialization and the kind of function that each department has, as well as the style exhibited by the leadership of the organization. In some cases, even the nature of the task confronting the leadership of the organization can have a bearing on the amount of free choice available to the subordinates within that organization. One of the principal dilemmas that confronts the leadership of any organization is whether or not to judge the fulfillment of a task more important than the maintenance of control (power) over those who are going to be achieving the goals or vice versa. Which, then, is more important—maintaining control or accomplishment?

Since the answer cannot be the same for every organization, it is a worthwhile exercise to present a schematic that will illustrate for us the many options open to a manager in choosing a leadership pattern. As shown in Figure 7-1, a continuum of power exists between the manager and his or her subordinates. This continuum can be constantly shifting depending on the nature of the task that confronts the organization, the amount of authority possessed by the leader, environmental factors, and perhaps even the traditions of leadership that the organization has already developed. For example, it would be difficult indeed for an authoritarian leader to come in on the heels of a predecessor who has believed in democratic decision making in his department. Thus, we can see that the democratic manager who tries to turn his department into a democracy in which most of the control would be exercised by the subordinates would be in for a rude shock indeed. He would find that the subordinates might very well yearn for the good old days when the boss acted like "the boss." Coming into a new position thus requires a great deal of perspicacity on your part. An abrupt change of style from that used by the previous leadership could be disastrous and result in a crisis of confidence as well as lowered morale from those on whom you must depend to get the job done. It is better to make any changes in leadership style slowly and cautiously, therefore, as sudden or abrupt change has only shock treatment value and little else to recommend it, especially when we want a smoothly running organization.

In Figure 7-1, which illustrates the relationship between a manager and his subordinates (nonmanagers), it is worthwhile noting that as the manager's decision-making authority decreases (as he consults more with his subordinates and has them play an ever larger role in the decision making), the area of freedom for the subordinates grows. There is thus a direct relationship between the manager and his subordinates that affects the amount of freedom each will have to make decisions. A manager can, of course, choose any of the many styles of leadership outlined in the diagram, but there are certain pitfalls and

Figure 7–1
Continuum of Manager-Nonmanager Behavior

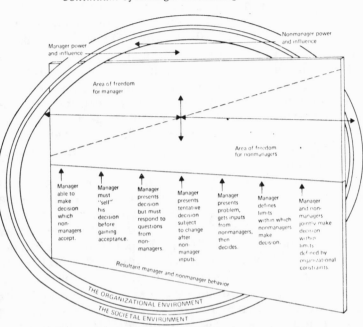

Source: Robert Tannenbaum and Warren H. Schmidt, "How to Choose a Leadership Pattern and a Retrospective Comment," *Harvard Business Review*, Vol. 51 (May–June 1973). Reprinted in *The Dimensions of Public Administration*, second ed., by Joseph A. Uveges, Jr., Holbrook Press, Inc., Boston, 1975.

problems that he or she ought to be aware of before rushing headlong into a management pattern. Some of these are:

1. Once the manager decides to declare himself a "democratic" leader and allow the subordinates a role in the decision-making process, the manager will be relinquishing some of his claim to authority. When this happens, or when authority is delegated over a long period of time, it is difficult to get that authority back. Therefore, much careful thought has to go into who you want to share in the decision

making, and just how much leeway you want that person or persons to have. It's very easy to give power away—and mighty difficult to get it back!

2. The manager must be guided by his own needs and demands. He can only permit his subordinates more freedom to consult with him if it is in agreement with his value system (perhaps he believes strongly in authority as a value) or if he has confidence in his subordinates' ability or if he feels comfortable (secure) within the framework of the decision-making scheme that he has constructed. Decision sharing is of little value if it is going to make the manager insecure.

3. The conditions under which the subordinates exist also play a role here. Do the subordinates have the .experience, the skills, the knowledge, and the collective wisdom with which to help make the decisions? Can they assume collective responsibility for bad decisions? Perhaps it is wiser to spend some time in education and discussion of what areas of responsibility the subordinates are expected to carry *before* there is any real sharing in decision making.

4. It must be made clear to subordinates that freedom to share in the decision making also means having the burden of responsibility for those decisions as well. Anyone can be a summer soldier; it takes courage to face the ice of winter!

5. Finally, there are organizational and other environmental restraints as the diagram shows. Perhaps the organization is traditionally hierarchical; then change must be introduced slowly. Perhaps the organization and its leadership is more concerned with power than with accomplishing tasks.

The nature of the organization will, of course, have a great deal to do with the amount of centralized authority that exists. A small organization that is labor intensive and concerned with production would probably have a much higher degree of centralized control by the manager(s), while an organization that depended more on individual effort and contribution would have a very high degree of decentralized control. The two most extreme examples would be a small manufacturing firm, where the piece work rate was the norm for the workers with emphasis on production (highly centralized) versus a "think tank" doing contract work for the government, each person working on his or her own research and conferring with the manager once a week or so (quite decentralized). In fact, I can recall an instance where a highly authoritarian manager in one of those think tanks lasted all of 3 weeks!

Choosing a leadership pattern is a difficult but necessary process. It must be done consciously and deliberately and only after taking many of the above-mentioned factors into account. But it is worth all the trouble because in the long run the right style of leadership will prove to be the most satisfying and productive for you, and thus will reflect to your credit.

Conflict, Cooperation, and Ideology

In Chapter 4, I discussed the value of conflict as a source of creativity for the individual within the organization. What about the organization itself? Is conflict on an intra-organizational level a healthy, desirable state of affairs? Can conflict be managed so that it remains a positive force in the life of the organization? What happens when the subgroups (departments, divisions) within the organization find themselves in conflict with the ideology (traditions, goals) of the organization? These and many other questions are at the root of the field of study known as organizational behavior. I have already suggested that organizations, like people, pass through three stages: youth, middle age, and old age; I should further suggest that organizations have emotional crises as well, and the health of the organization depends to a great extent on how well its "emotional" problems are resolved.

Pete Estes, President of General Motors, gave an interesting example of intraorganizational conflict. As head of the Pontiac division of General Motors before he became president, he was, by his own admission, out to make Pontiac the best division in General Motors. Then Estes was transferred to the Oldsmobile division, which he felt was quite a letdown—something like going to work for your competitor. Nevertheless, he soon buckled down again to make the Oldsmobile division the best of the divisions in the General Motors family. Finally, Estes was tapped to become the chief executive of the entire organization. When an interviewer asked Estes how he felt about heading up all of those competing divisions, he had very mixed feelings. But he rationalized them by saying that after all, General Motors was still one big, happy family, while those other companies (Ford, Chrysler) were the *real* enemy. Pete Estes was simply demonstrating how group loyalties can be transferred and broadened considerably. His "in group" complexes at Pontiac and Oldsmobile found themselves quickly transferred to the entire company. It is worthwhile noting in this connection that there always has to be an "in group" expressing some degree of hostility to the outside world and in competition with other outside groups as well. So the first thing we have to learn about intraorganizational conflict is that it can be healthy and should be regarded as normal. However, it must always be managed, for conflict can lead to hostility and hostility to aggression, and that's where the trouble can start in an organization.

Within any organization, there is competition—competition for prestige, competition for power, competition for a place in the hierarchy, i.e. a place in the sun. Thus, many writers on the subject have described organizational interplay as "political," a kind of nasty word that connotes something akin to barroom brawling to many. Yet, the competition is there and it is keen indeed. The problem is to preserve the competition while at the same time keeping the politics as clean as possible—no jabs below the belt. While that's easier said than done, it is indispensable to the emotional well-being of any organization, and becomes the immediate responsibility of the organization's leadership. Pete Estes or any other executive leader of a large organization has the responsibility of seeing to it that the various competing divisions in his organization remain productive as well as competitive. Politics within the organization need not be dirty or manipulative in order to aid the progress of the organization. Every leader of a group builds a constituency for himself or herself. These constitutencies contain loyal followers who perceive their leader to be operating in the best interests of their group. When these perceptions are good, and when their chief can deliver certain fringe benefits, rewards from higher productivity, or perhaps some special recognition from the parent company for their achievements, loyalty to the chief will follow, and morale will be considerably heightened. When, on the other hand, the chief cannot perform in such an excellent manner, morale will drop, and with it production. Such are the psychological facts of organizational life. Thus, the leader's principal task is to play two kinds of roles:

1. To obtain the highest kind of group cohesion that he can within his department, and to keep down the level of infighting by consultation, negotiation, and bargaining.
2. To represent his department to the higher levels of decision making, and to fight for both his position and, consequently, the position of his department so as to remain prominent within the hierarchy of the organization.

The second goal, as described above, is playing politics with the external forces in the organization. The principal way in which this is done is by forming coalitions with other forces. In general, we could say that the successful leader is one who is perceived by his followers to be most powerful in the organizational hierarchy. Such a leader will be perceived to be the kind who will do a better job in looking out for his group (providing better conditions or better pay) than one who is less powerful. Coalitions are simply groups of executives that work together to solve problems, rather than spend their days and nights worrying about mutual hostility or backbiting. Abraham Zaleznik points out:

> The formal organizational structure implements a coalition among key executives. The forms differ, and the psychological significance of various coalitions also differs. But no organization can function without a consolidation of power in the relationship of a central figure with his select group. The coalition need not exist between the chief executive and his immediate subordinates or staff.... The failure to establish a coalition within the executive structure of an organization can result in severe problems, such as paralysis in the form of inability to make decisions and to evaluate performance, and in-fighting and overt rivalry within the executive group.[3]

What Professor Zaleznik is saying is that politics can and should be an orderly procedure. Competition is taken for granted—may the best and the brightest win for the good of the company—but the process need not be destructive and chaotic. But, alas, such is not always the case. There are forces in the manager as well as in the organization that lend themselves to collusion (plotting, scheming) that can be attributed directly to the vagaries of the human condition, not the least of which is paranoia.

A coalition represents a collection of persons with power. This coalition can use their power for constructive purposes or for destructive purposes. Two examples that illustrate both points are given below:

> Example 1. The ABC Manufacturing Corporation has a marketing and sales department as well as a product development division. The president is uncertain as to whether or not he should provide a larger budget to sales and marketing or to products development. An increase in budget for either division would mean hiring more personnel, increasing activity, etc. In a *coalition* situation, the president would arrange meetings where open and frank discussions of the issues and the evidence would be presented by both sides. Other departments of the corporation would be involved in contributing

their opinions as well. Thus, there would be an atmosphere of cooperation as well as healthy, nondestructive competition.
Example 2. The XYZ Corporation is just in the process of setting up a new engineering division. This new division will cause a drop in the budgets of the older divisions, yet all of the executives of the corporation think that a new engineering division will make the corporation more viable, and produce more business in the long run. An *unhealthy, collusive* atmosphere would result if the executives of the threatened divisions went behind the back of the president, to try to get the board of directors to overrule or even fire the president. There would be little or no discussion of the impending change; perhaps the president would be rigid and unyielding, and fail to understand the points of view of the threatened divisions. In this case, the threatened executives, anxious to defend their divisions *against* the interests of the corporation, will become destructive of the health of the organization.

In both cases as illustrated above, there is a largely unstructured situation. The first example is solved by the politics of pragmatic problem solving and persuasion. The second is resolved by conspiracy; hence it is irrational, and will be destructive of the goals of the organization. While it is true that each department executive is anxious to protect his own turf, it must also be remembered that the general interests of the organization must be protected at all costs. Each executive must therefore be reminded by the chief executive officer that only rational coalitions that utilize the best abilities of their members will be allowed. The first example shows awareness on the part of the executives that general health is most important; the second example shows the dominance of narrow, selfish interests, presided over by a stubborn, rigid father figure.

Ideology is the engine that drives an organization. It energizes it, gives it spirit and soul, and provides it with a reason for existence. Ideology consists of both goals and values. Hence, an organization's ideology will combine its objectives with the kind of method that it deems most appropriate for reaching those goals. Generally speaking, the individual in the organization is expected to share in that organization's values. That is, he or she is expected to identify with the ideological values of the organization. A person who works for a corporation that manufactures bottles (nondeposit, nonreturn), for example, would hardly be considered in consonance with his or her organization's ideology if he or she supported antibottle legislation.

The above may be considered a rather simplistic example, but in reality strikes at the heart of the matter. As a manager, you will be expected to make the goals of your organization *your* goals as well. Sometimes this causes conflict with the external world as well as internal conflict. When Ralph Nader first began a crusade against the manufacturers of cars that he suggested were hazardous to the driving public, officials of one of the large automobile manufacturers began a campaign to discredit Nader by casting doubts on Nader's reputation and character, and by hiring private detectives to dig up any unfavorable or negative information that they could on Mr. Nader. They not only drew a blank, but they wound up making an embarrassing public apology to Ralph Nader. It was this incident that probably assured the passage of legislation that ultimately regulated the automobile manufacturing industry for the first time in history. Those executives were highly motivated, imbued with the spirit of their organization, but they were so overwhelmed by their own ideology that they lost sight of the ultimate goals of their organization—a good public image.

An organization's ideology, therefore, cannot be seen as rigid or unyielding to internal or external pressures. Indeed, those organization executives who behave in this fashion are doing their parent a great injustice. Compare any great corporation's ideology of today with its ideology of 20 years ago, and you will quickly agree that there has indeed been a great change in the goals and values of that organization. In some cases, it has been as a result of economic or public pressure. In others, it may have been an answer to internal needs. In any case, the forces for qualitative change have caused profound changes in the ideology of the organization. What I am really saying is that as a manager, you *can* have it both ways. You can retain your own ideology while at the same time becoming imbued with the spirit of the organization that you work for. When and if you sense a need for a shift in the organization's ideology (values), you must then exercise your leadership ability by persuading the organization to turn itself around. This can be done by sound, rational, and persuasive logic. And it is ultimately rewarding in the extreme. In fact, there probably has never been a comparable time in history when organizations, public as well as private, were under so much ideological stress. This brings us to a fourth and final concept, that of social responsibility

Social Responsibility

In the past decade, a revolutionary development has been stalking executives in all kinds of organizations. It is the responsibility revolution. Agencies, corporations, and public service organizations are being strongly affected by new laws and new trends, all of which are calling the organization more strongly than ever to account for its action. And, of course, it is the executive who has to play the role of defender. A recent article in the *New York Times* points out:

> The executive begins by defending his company against charges of pollution before a skeptical city council. Then he rushes to meet with angry representatives of minority groups who complain of employment discrimination. After that, he fields rumors that his plant is just about to lay off hundreds of workers. Just as a horrid day is about to end, an explosion hits the plant, and in the resulting chaos, the executive must deal with TV cameramen and reporters clamoring to cover the story. . . .
>
> Chief executives, who often have backgrounds in marketing or finance, find themselves spending 25 percent or more of their time dealing with the press, Congress or pressure groups. Often, the chief executive is at a loss on how to handle his role.[4]

These pressures on the executives have created a bonanza for the public relations specialists, and many public relations firms are now specializing in helping to solve crises in relationships with the external world. No organization is immune from these kinds of problems. For example, government agencies are besieged as never before by the fact that government archives have had to be open to public view. The Freedom of Information Act, first passed by Congress in 1966, but amended in 1974, has guaranteed public access to virtually every document except those which are concerned with national security. More than ever before, citizens are suing their government for everything from radiation damage to discrimination on the job. And many of them are winning cases that a formerly impregnable government would never concede. Government executives are rapidly discovering that they must have a sense of responsibility to the general public as well.

Business corporations have also faced great challenges in the past two decades. A generation that has been weaned on Naderism and consumerism is no longer going to be a passive sitting duck for the business community. Many authorities have described this generation as the most litigious in history, and judging by the number of lawsuits, they are probably right.

In addition, regulatory agencies, such as the Environmental Protection Agency, the Consumer Product Safety Commission, or the Office of Safety and Health Administration, are placing a tremendous burden on the corporation executive. It does not seem likely that this burden is going to lessen very much, despite the promises of several Presidents to reduce the burden of regulation. In addition, there are other new requirements such as Affirmative Action. (As of this writing, the Supreme Court has come down hard on the side of special treatment of minorities in corporation training programs. For example, see *Weber v. Kaiser Industries.*) The corporation is also assuming more responsibility for its employees as well. It is offering everything from psychiatric counseling to assistance in job placement for the employee who has been terminated.

Public service institutions similarly have been made more aware of their social responsibilities in recent times. Hospitals can no longer be selective as to whom they treat. Moreover, hospitals have been under fire as the chief culprit in spiraling health-care costs. Academic institutions have come under great criticism for investing their endowment funds in business corporations that maintain ties with countries that are perceived as racist (South Africa, for example) by student bodies.

As a budding executive, the implications of these new trends should make it clear to you that one of your chief tasks will be to become and remain as well-informed as possible. Being well-informed about your organization's affairs, your specialty, or even your marketplace is simply not enough anymore. Today's executive has got to be aware of all developments that may affect him or his organization. Shrewd guessing is based mostly on good, accurate information, and the informed person is going to be the one with the better intuition. Our second rule, then, is: *There are five factors that are common to all organizations, and that must be regarded by you as normal processes. These are: different leadership styles, conflict, politics, the organization's ideological aspirations, and the growing need for a sense of social responsibility.*

THE EMPIRES OF THE FUTURE ARE THE EMPIRES OF THE MIND

These words were spoken by Sir Winston Churchill in an address at Harvard University in 1943. How prophetic they were can be seen by the changes that modern civilization has undergone as a result of human ingenuity and creativity.

What will be the future of organizations? As an executive, your work and its character will largely be determined by what will happen over the course of your working lifetime. One of the ways in which we can determine what the future will look like is by studying present trends. Recent changes in the structure and function of organizations can give us some positive clues, and should provide us with a road map whose markings may not be exact, but which can point out certain general directions.

First, the science known as *cybernetics* will become a major factor in organizational life. Cybernetics, from the Greek, means "self-steering," and ever since it was first popularized by the late Norbert Wiener and others over 30 years ago, has increasingly become part of our environment. Cybernetics goes beyond the process known as automation because Cybernetics means the self-actualizing, thinking, and self-regulating organization. Industrial plants that are now run by computers are good examples of Cybernetics. The only flaw in the example is that these plants are still subject to human control and to human interference. Visualize, if you will, a plant that produces products that is not only completely automated, but projects supply and demand for its product and may even change the style of the product after predicting new fashion trends. All of this would be done without human intervention. Cybernetics will thus usher in the age of the thinking and planning machine, and is very much a part of the future. The introduction of the computer, the semiconductor, and EDP (electronic data processing) have revolutionized management. Cybernetics will take that revolution one step further, and will ultimately replace most middle management jobs that are now concerned with routine work. Cybernetics will ultimately make it possible for society to produce most of its needs without human intervention, and although this is still in the future, it is becoming increasingly clear that much more emphasis is going to be placed on research, problem solving, and the use of creative imagination than ever before. The age of Cybernetics has already dawned. Few corporate decisions are made today without some kind of computer analysis, and the full automation of the productive forces of society are just now beginning. As a manager therefore, your life will be far from dull or routine and will be more involved than ever with creative work.

Second, organizations will become larger and much more prolific than they are at present. I have already alluded to the recent development of the multinational corporation. It seems clear that the corporation of the future will be more of a conglomerate than ever before. Many writers on the subject have suggested that the corporation will proliferate so much that it will abandon the usual hierarchical structure that is still typical of many such organizations. Instead, the hierarchical structure will be replaced by a series of smaller, segmented horizontal structures, each representing a department or a division. There will be far greater autonomy for each division, and the chief executive officer will find himself presiding less, and acting more as a liaison. What this means is not only a diminution of authority for the chief executive, but far greater autonomy for the divisions, and for the managers of those divisions as well. Thus, such fragmentation will produce the need for more managers and will make for more complex organizations than we presently know.

Third, the world will become a much more interdependent place than it has ever been—and that goes for international trade as well. The nations of the West (the Atlantic Community, as it used to be called) will become more closely knit, and will see themselves as much more of an economic unit than heretofore. One simply has to witness such developments as the creation of a Parliament of Europe, the rapid expansion of the European Common Market, and the beginnings of a common front against the oil cartels to believe that closer ties will develop and that economic as well as political integration are very much in the cards. The missing link, of course, is the developing countries and the communist nations (some of these are synonymous). Most of them are "champing at the bit" for increased trade relations with the West and an increase in the importation of Western technology. So the world that has shrunk so much already is on the verge of shrinking some more.

Fourth, there will be an increasing need for specialists, or as Peter Drucker calls them "knowledge workers,"[5] who will have to grapple with the problems of technological innovation and change. These specialists will need support systems (financing, organizational framework) to do their work. Moreover, there will have to be an easy, informal interface between the manager and the specialist. So the manager will have to become much more flexible and adaptable. Certainly, he will be required to maintain the type of atmosphere in which specialists can operate with the greatest amount of freedom.

If mankind makes it safely through the twentieth century, the organization will have to undergo profound change. Human nature, of course, will change much more slowly. The future, therefore, has to be seen as no more than a compromise between the vagaries of human nature and the demands of the technological revolution that is already upon us. The need, however, for wisdom, human understanding, and intuition are going to remain quite necessary. Why? Because we are still focusing on *Homo sapiens* as the final object of all our endeavors. We are not in advanced technology to please machines; we are in it to please man, and man will remain the primary consideration. Therefore, if you train yourself in the skills of managing people with understanding, there'll always be a place for you. Our third rule, then, is: *Organizations will undergo profound changes in the next 20 or 30 years. Managers' human skills, however, will always be required.*

SUMMARY

While all organizations have some similar traits—internal conflict, the need to constantly adjust, and organizational problems—they are each unique. There are three basic kinds of organizations; namely, government agencies, private corporations, and public service institutions. The government agencies are funded by the taxpayers and have no competition or markets to capture. The private corporations are funded by the shareholders who hire the managers with the expectation that they will produce profits (dividends) for the shareholders. The public service institutions are charitable trusts, and fill in the gray areas between government agencies and the private sector.

There are many factors that determine the direction and character of an organization. Among these are: the amount and kinds of controls (centralized or decentralized); the kinds of internal conflict that the organization has, and how conflicts are resolved within the organization; the political climate of the organization and its effect on the organization's emotional well-being; and the nature of the process of cooperation by the organization's executives, known as coalitions.

Every organization has its ideology, and conflicts can result when an executive's personal ideals are in conflict with those of his organization. This will call for some soul searching on his part.

Today's organizations are being forced more than ever before to answer to the public. The idea of social responsibility, although fairly new, is rapidly becoming a significant factor at all levels.

The future of organizations will largely be determined by the needs of a world that shrinks more each year and, consequently, is becoming more interdependent economically as well as politically. As each decade passes, the world becomes more complicated technologically, and these new factors will place growing demands for more creative energy on executives than ever before. Nevertheless, the human skills will always be an important asset to the managers of the future.

EXERCISES FOR CHAPTER 7

1. Arrange to attend a stockholders' meeting of one of the large corporations. These are held once a year in the large cities of the United States. You can probably get in as an observer without much difficulty. If you know someone (friend or relative) who owns stock in that corporation, they could probably get you in. Record your reactions to the ideology, goals, and interests of the corporation's

executives. Also, record reactions of the stockholders. What areas seemed most important to the executives? To the stockholders?

2. Join a public interest or consumer organization. Find out what motivates these groups and the people in them. Do you find yourself in sympathy with their goals? Find out how these groups relate to the government, the corporation, and to the general public.

3. Do some volunteer work for a public charitable trust. Get to know something about how they are funded and what their problems and motivations are. Incidentally, since most corporations are extremely sensitive about their public image, they are quite anxious to promote people who are involved in community organizations to executive status.

4. Take a tour of an automated industrial plant. Many corporations allow guided tours, and if you have never seen an automated production line, you should. It's very educational!

5. Using the diagram on page 179, develop some areas of decision sharing that might be used with more freedom for the subordinates. This could be done where you work or perhaps where a friend or relative works. Try to develop a new model for that organization that will provide new relationships and consequently new patterns of decision making.

NOTES

1. *Public Administration Times,* July 15, 1979.

2. Peter F. Drucker, "Managing The Public Service Institution," *The Public Interest,* No. 33, Fall, 1973.

3. Abraham Zaleznik, "Power and Politics in Organizational Life," in *Harvard Business Review: On Human Relations.* Harper & Row, New York, 1979. p. 382.

4. *The New York Times,* July 29, 1979.

5. Peter F. Drucker, *Management.* Harper & Row, New York, 1974. p. 30.

8

Imagination

$\mathcal{I}$ met a banker who told me a rather extraordinary story as follows: The banker was stationed in one of the countries of the Middle East, and attended one of the many cocktail parties that are continually part of the scene. At the cocktail party, he met a Soviet financial official with whom he had previously been friendly. As they strode out to the balcony to admire the beautiful sunset, conversation turned to capturing that beautiful scene with a camera, and of course, the two men began discussing cameras. The banker told the Soviet official, "Of course, with a Polaroid camera, you are sure of what you're taking because the picture develops itself on the spot." The Soviet official replied, "Come on, now—stop pulling my leg. You know there's no such thing as a camera that develops its own pictures instantly. I wish you people would stop treating us like country bumpkins. We're a sophisticated people, you know." The Russian was incensed. The banker protested it was so, and finally drove home and returned with his

Polaroid camera. When he took a picture of the Soviet official and it came out fully developed and recognizable, the official could not conceal his amazement: "So, it really is true!" he said.

Imagination and the ability to use it—these qualities are the secrets of Western success and progress. It is obvious that the stultifying atmosphere of socialist countries retards the creative thinker to the point that even sophisticated, worldly people such as the Soviet official cannot use their imaginations with much success. We Americans have long taken pride in our ability to invent, to innovate, to create. There used to be a saying, "Give any American boy a screwdriver, and he can fix anything." But even the United States is having difficulties these days, and the competition is keen. What the Japanese and the European nations are doing in the way of creating new machines, new methods, and new technology is becoming more of a challenge to us each day. The key to economic survival, more than ever before, is the ability to create, to innovate, and to use our minds to develop new tools, new products and new ways of doing things. A recent article in "Newsweek" points out:

> As other industrialized nations such as West Germany and Japan pump more and more money into their R & D, America's command of the world technology market grows more precarious.[1]

Thus, the great dilemma for America has been to rediscover that very same quality that made us a great nation to begin with—the ability to create. This need is more than a challenge for the nation—it's a challenge for you as well, because the one real asset that you'll be bringing with you to your executive position will be creativity. You may gag at the thought and say, "But I'm not a creative person!" In fact, I think you'll have changed your mind by the time you finish this chapter. First, let's look at what creativity —the ability to develop and use a healthy imagination—is.

THE EUREKA COMPLEX

Most of us suffer from the illusion that creative people are eccentrics who suffer from absent-mindedness and make great discoveries at some inspired moment. Indeed, American folklore is filled with just such themes as the eccentric inventor or the mad scientist. But that is a myth and quite far from the truth. In fact, a great deal has been learned about creativity, what it is, how it is developed, and what kinds of people are more creative than others. First, you should be disabused of the notion that people are born "creative" or have good imaginations and that these are qualities that are inherited, not developed. According to Alex Osborn, the father of the "brainstorming" technique and a founder of the Creative Education Foundation:

> That this talent (creativity) can be developed is beyond question. Psychologists long ago accepted the tenet that any primary ability can be trained—that even an average potential can be developed by exercise.[2]

Osborn is quite right. You will never develop your imagination by sitting on it. You must exercise it. The Greek Philosopher Aristotle said more than 2,000 years ago, "For imagining lies within our power whenever we wish."[3] Moreover, get rid of the notion that creative imagination is only for the artist or for the scientist. It's for everyone. As an executive, you'll develop your imagination and creativity, and you'll have it working actively for you. Everyone, regardless of his role in life, can be creative. The housewife who thinks up a new recipe, the general who creates a new strategy, the Congressman who develops a new piece of legislation, the sales manager who develops a new sales strategy—these are human beings who are exercising their creative capacities. And they're finding out that life can be a lot more challenging and a great deal more fun when they behave creatively. So creative behavior is not just a saving feature of Western society—it's a saving feature for yourself and will keep you alert and interested. You should always have the attitude that there must be a better (cheaper, easier, more efficient, prettier, more pleasing) way of doing something. If you keep looking at your job from that perspective, you'll find yourself becoming a creative executive very quickly. Furthermore, exercising those imaginative and creative powers of yours will become richly rewarding, both materially and psychologically, because you'll be solving problems that other people who are too lazy to use their imaginations are unable to solve. The mind is a muscle; it needs exercise, and once those muscles are sinewy, they can be applied to many other problems with increasing ease. Let's now take a look at what creative behavior is, and what creative thinking can do for the individual.

How Do You Get There From Here?

Most authorities are agreed that creative imagination is responsible for developing new and possibly better solutions to existing problems. While imagination involves the ability to recall (ideas, images), creative imagination means being able to synthesize something new and perhaps unique from bits and pieces of information that are old. Creativity also involves the need to be able to *visualize.* The process of synthesis is not easy to describe, but it is essential to creative behavior.

The first step is, of course, being presented with a problem. For the artist or the scientist in the laboratory, those problems are his or her daily diet. For others, problems must be first discovered, and that means becoming *motivated* to want to constantly improve conditions or methods. Thus, we must first find the problems that we are going to present ourselves with to be solved. If we are lazy or nonchalant about our responsibilities, we obviously will find few or no problems at all. So *motivation* is really the first key since it moves us to act. After we have discovered the problem to be solved, then we begin a process of analysis that will not only dissect the problem but will present us with large numbers of statistics and facts about the problem. Finally, we synthesize a solution to the problem. That's where the "Aha!" or "Eureka!" comes in if it's to come in at all. The process of discovering a new solution to an existing problem is not really automatic. It requires a number of complex steps. We can describe these steps as follows:

Five Steps to Creative Problem Solving

1. Fluency by bombardment
2. Gestation
3. Deliberation
4. Suspended judgment and testing
5. Solution

The first step, *fluency by bombardment,* is an initial means of attacking the problem, once the motivation for seeking a solution has been established. The mind has to be opened to a continuous flow of ideas. Some of these ideas may seem at the outset to be wistful or foolish, but at the earliest stages, no idea should be considered too foolish to risk thinking about. Since the brain can only react to the amount of data presented to it, the beginning phase of any flow of ideas is to collect as much material as possible, that is, as many facts about the problem that we can collect. Thus, not only should you carefully describe the problem in as detailed a fashion as possible, *and in writing,* but you should collect as many *facts* about the problem as you can and put those *facts* in writing as well. Now you have a complete record. The problem has been stated and you have facts about the problem, its history, its consequences, its effects, and what its solution might mean. What you are now doing is establishing a creative climate and you are also setting the stage for some fairly deliberate thinking about the problem. You are also destroying whatever mental blocks you may have had about the problem that caused you to refuse to look at it or consider it *as* a problem before.

During this first phase of fluency by bombardment, there is also another curious psychological effect. Our search for facts will also begin the processes of association in our brains as well, and lead to a continuous relationship between the facts about the problem and the flow of ideas that will relate the problem morphologically, sequentially, and familiarly.

By morphological analysis, we mean that the problem is going to be reduced to some kind of structure so that we can deal with it as a visual object. At the same time, we are going to establish certain boundaries (parameters) to that structure, so that we shall not have to be distracted by an indefinite number of variable factors that may have little bearing on the problem at hand. Morphological analysis is a means of imposing some degree of discipline in our attack on the problem. While a free flow of ideas (fluency) is highly encouraged, that flow will be contained in the structure surrounding the problem so that extraneous and irrelevant material will be avoided. One way to do this is to construct, on paper, a diagram or picture of the problem. An example of morphological analysis is given below:

> *The problem:* A manufacturer of foodstuffs is faced with a choice between using wholesale food brokers to handle his product or setting up his own distribution outlets and sales forces. *Morphological analysis* would mean that the manufacturer would actually construct models of both systems. These models would then present visually how each system could operate, and what variable factors one could expect in each system. Models would also show costs and benefits of each system in a highly visible way, much the same way that an architect prepares a model for a building that he intends to design.

Thus, working models give us a picture of the proposed system at work, and at the same time keep us focused on the structural problems as well. In brief, morphological analysis leaves less to the imagination than other forms of analysis because it gives us an opportunity to *see* what exists as against what *might* exist. The one great advantage that this system has is that it continually forces us to keep looking at the model that we have constructed, and this tends to keep out irrelevant or distracting material.

Sequential analysis of a problem is a second but different way of looking at the problem. One method is using a checklist. Checklists can be specialized or generalized, but they perform a valuable service because they give us an orderly, empirical method of analysis that will leave no stone unturned. In short, what we are searching for is an exhaustive list of attributes. There are several kinds of checklists described below:

1. Attribute checklist:

   (a) Describe what the problem feels like.
   (b) Describe what the problem looks like. Shape? Size?
   (c) Describe the problem's salient *good* features.
   (d) Describe the problem's salient *bad* features.
   (e) In short, what qualities does the problem now possess? Describe these qualities in detail.

2. Generalized checklist: What can we do with the present product or condition?

   (a) Modify it? Change its color, size, shape, importance?
   (b) Magnify it? Bigger? More Time? More Frequency?
   (c) Minimize it? Smaller? Less Time? Less Frequency?
   (d) Rearrange things? Break them up? Reverse the order?
   (e) Recombine? New combination? New proportions? Combine new ideas? Reverse things? Combine roles?

Starting out an analysis of a problem with a checklist that is as exhaustive as you can make it will provide you with an easy way of covering all of the territory, enabling you to review everything and forcing your mind to be sure that you have covered every possible avenue of approach. The checklist approach is an excellent way of doing this.

There is an old saying that "familiarity breeds contempt." In this case, familiarity with the problem will breed ideas instead! The familiar technique means quite simply learning as much about the problem and its environment as you possibly can. For example, in the problem given above concerning the manufacturer of foodstuffs, the familiarity technique would be in making the decision maker thoroughly familiar with the characteristics of the market, the characteristics of the consumers, the nature of food brokerage, the nature of retail sales, the procedures followed by other food manufacturers, i.e. do they sell the same type of product? What has been their experience? Perhaps a study of regional characteristics or even a study of the marketing techniques used in other countries might be considered. Obviously, a great deal of study, time, and attention will have to be given over to the problem, but the payoff will be well worth the effort invested. Certainly the investigator will become one of the local experts on this type of problem.

All of the above techniques are a means of getting started on fluency by bombardment. They can be used either singly or together, but they will act as a catalyst for your mind to get you to think about the problem, and to generate as great a flow of ideas as possible. Many authorities have suggested that there be as much open-mindedness when considering alternatives as possible. We have already considered, in Chapter 5, the "brainstorming" technique as a means of generating activity and ideas in a group conference. The fluency of ideas is a brainstorming type of technique that can be used by the individual.

Finally, there is *serendipity*. The word serendipity is taken from a fable that was created by Horace Walpole, entitled *The Three Princes of Serendip.*[4] These three princes lived in a far-off legendary land, and were always making unusual but happy discoveries of things that they were not really looking for. They would go searching for one thing, and come up with another. Thus, making happy and unexpected discoveries by accident can be one of the byproducts of just *looking,* as the Princes of Serendip found out. A steady stream of ideas—quantity—is what will produce unexpected and sometimes fortuitous results. Many great and important discoveries have been made unexpectedly while the discoverer was looking for something else that was completely irrelevant to the problem at hand. So keep in mind that *serendipity* is another creative technique.

Gestation is the second step in creative problem solving. Unlike frequency, gestation will require much more patience and time. Gestation is a biological term that means carrying an embryo from the time of conception to the time of birth. What better way is there to describe the process by which an idea takes shape and form until it finally emerges from the mental womb—the mind? After a period of rather frenzied activity and concentration, collecting facts and data, building structures, etc., the time comes to take a rest and allow the rapid flow of ideas to gestate. During this period of incubation, the ideas that have already developed will begin to float around in our subconscious; they will take root and begin to develop almost effortlessly. In fact, some find that they develop almost of their own accord. They have their own inertial energy, it seems. At any rate, gestation is an important part of the creative process and must not be overlooked because any good idea needs a period of reflection and growth if it is at all worthwhile.

During the gestation period, we deliberately place all of our thoughts and ideas on the "back burner" of our minds and turn our attention to other things or activities. By some process that is still not well understood, the ideas continue to simmer and cook, *but they do not come to a boil,* not yet! For these ideas to come to a boil prematurely would be analogous to opening an oven door too soon and watching a cake collapse—something every cook dreads. So slow and deliberate cooking is as important to the gestation of ideas as it is to the baking of cakes. Curiously enough, it has been the experience of most creative people that when the right idea is ready, it will birth itself. It will pop into your conscious mind with what appears to be no effort at all.

How do we facilitate this important process of gestation? By the process known as relaxation. There are several methods used by famous people that are instructive. Sir Winston Churchill used to relax by painting or bricklaying. He was also fond of taking baths as a method of inducing gestation. Franklin Roosevelt used to relax his mind by reading detective stories. One of the more popular modern methods is relaxing by meditation. The recent attraction of meditation for many professional and executive people is not simply a current fad. These people have found that meditation has a "cleansing" effect on the mind, and have found that the creative processes flow much more easily after meditation. It has also been discovered that stress and tension have a deleterious effect on the creative mind as well.[5]

Others find relaxation and distraction through more active pastimes such as jogging, playing handball or tennis, etc. (I have found that I can frequently come up with new ideas or a fresh approach to a problem that has been bothering me after jogging for 2 or 3 miles. Joseph Heller, a best-selling novelist, also has related the same kind of experiences after jogging.) The point is that after periods of intense concentration and generating a flow of ideas, you must then deliberately allow time for those ideas to incubate, and then the *right* idea will begin to emerge; the pieces of the puzzle will fall into place, and you'll be well on the way toward solution.

The third step in the creative process is *deliberation.* It is during this stage that we begin the processing of the ideas that have emerged during the gestation stage. At this point, the ideas that have emerged are tentative and may even seem to be trite or silly. But this is not the stage at which ideas should be discarded. Instead, ideas now should be tested against reality, and we should begin a deeper search for even more ideas. For example, the Gordon technique, named for W. J. Gordon of Arthur D. Little, Inc., exposes the ideas generated by group thinking to underlying concepts rather than attempting to restrict thinking to the problem at hand. Here is the method:

> The group attacks the underlying concept of the problem rather than the problem itself. For example, if a new principle for a can opener is wanted, the group leader introduces the general subject of *opening.* When the client desires a new workshop item, the subject of *hobbies* is raised. When a cutting device is wanted, the subject of *severing* is introduced.
>
> Underlying concepts are explored at length, and subjects are examined from many angles—social and economic as well as mechanical.
>
> Out of these sessions have come a number of radically new ideas. . . . Participants, most of them engineers—claim that concentrating on the underlying concept has two advantages.
>
> It prevents early closure on the problem. That is, it keeps participants from thinking they have already seen the obvious answer.
>
> It encourages radical applications of old techniques. For example, when one client wanted a new type of lawnmower and the subject of severing was discussed, participants went so far afield as to consider the principle of the acetylene torch. Had the specific objective of a lawnmower been considered, in all likelihood their minds would never have made such a leap. . . . [6]

A. D. Little Company is a research firm that handles problems for all kinds of clients. One scientist I knew who worked for them was given the assignment to find out what makes one brand of scotch whiskey taste different from another. His answer, after many months of research, was the amount of fusel oil in scotch determined its flavor and taste. Much to his own surprise as well as that of his clients, it was discovered that age had little to do with flavor or taste—just the amount of fusel oil.

Deliberation means, therefore, that we must continue a free-wheeling association of the ideas that have already emerged, and attempt to push these ideas as far in our conscious minds as possible. Only in that way will we be able to stretch our imaginations and our minds as far as possible. The generation of ideas must, therefore, be a never ending process—the more the better.

The fourth stage in the creative problem-solving process is *suspended judgment and testing.* During this stage, we are allowing the ideas that we have come up with time to sink in, to digest, even as we allow our digestive processes time to digest a good meal. By the same token, we are also becoming involved in testing the various ideas that have sprung from our subconscious minds. This period of suspended judgment is very important to the creative procedure because it forces us to become objective, to stand away and take a more circumspect look at our ideas, before we make any mistakes in judgment. There are also several other reasons why suspending judgement is a good idea. For one thing, the problem may resolve itself, given a little time. For another, the conditions that precipitated the problem may have changed, and with a change in the environment, the problem could assume a new quality altogether.

There is yet another reason for suspending judgment on the ideas that you have developed for a while. This reason is buried in the field of Gestalt psychology. Too much proximity to the problem causes the individual to lose his control over the problem, and further, causes him to lose his objectivity as well. The vital point about Gestalt psychology is that Gestalt makes us see how things fit together, how they pattern themselves, and how they finally emerge as a complete, picture (that's where the "Aha!" comes in). We can only get the complete picture if we have some kind of psychological distance from the problem (objectivity). Otherwise we shall not be able to see the forest on account of the trees. One easy way to suspend judgment, of course, is simply to divert your mind with other activities for a while, and then come back to the possible solutions of the problem. It is amazing how a refreshed mind can attack a problem with renewed vigor. The mind is not refreshed so much by entertainment or rest (escapism) as it is by other activities within the framework of your job.

Finally, the ideas that you have been digesting and considering must also be tested. Testing is an essential step in coming to any solution of a problem. Many large organizations conduct field tests of ideas before they swing into large advertising campaigns, for example. New models of products are often tested like new recipes. Intuition and hunches may play an important role in the development of a solution to a problem, but without testing, they can be worthless. All hypotheses have to be tested against reality.

The fifth and final step is the *solution* to the problem. Some call this the period of illumination, referring to the old cartoons that pictured a light bulb going on in the head of the discoverer. Happily, the problem that was to be solved is now solved. Bear in mind, however, that the solution may produce other problems or that the solution may be short-lived. Nothing lasts forever, and you must be able to get those creative juices flowing again at any moment. Our first rule, then, is: *Anyone can be creative provided he or she is motivated, enthusiastic, and follows the five-step method of problem solving: fluency, gestation, deliberation, suspended judgment and testing, and solution.*

Road Blocks to Creativity

There are hindrances to creativity that have to be guarded against. These hazards will reduce your creative output, if you allow them to. For each hazard, however, there is a remedy, so let's present them in that fashion:

Hindrances to Creativity

1. Too much logic cramps or inhibits the imagination, especially in the early stages of ideational activity (fluency). Throwing out ideas early because they're "too silly" is even more foolish than the "silly" ideas. *Do not prejudge ideas!*

2. Rigidity hampers the flow of creative ideas. We are all creatures of habit, but unless we can "let ourselves go" a little bit, the flow of ideas is again relegated to a thin trickle. One way to change your approach to thinking, therefore, is to change a few of your habits. Try doing things a little differently, and you'll find yourself becoming more flexible, hence, more receptive to those new ideas as they float in.

3. Timidity also slows down productive ideas. Many a good idea was lost because the originator of the idea was embarrassed to present it for fear of bringing ridicule upon himself. We all have certain personal standards by which we live. Sometimes a person with a good idea discourages himself because he feels that his idea may not be worthy of him or may change people's opinion of him. At other times, criticism of an idea (rejection) by others may cause him to withdraw his idea. Many early ideas, including the automobile and the airplane were rejected as impractical when they first appeared. Perseverance is most certainly the antidote for timidity.

4. Self-discouragement. This may be fostered by a poor self-image or by failure to solve a problem, or both. They can become mutually reinforcing. Just remember that some of the world's greatest ideas and their creators have faced intense discouragement. When Chopin arrived in Vienna in the 1830s, he found the entire city driven crazy by the latest fad, waltzes, and consequently not at all interested in his music. What would have happened if he allowed himself to be defeated is, happily, interesting only as speculation. Edwin L. Drake, a retired railroad conductor, was hired by a group of businessmen to see how oil could be extracted from the ground in Titusville, Pa. After digging a pit in the ground in May, 1858, with discouraging results, Drake sat disconsolately staring at his stovepipe hat, when the idea of sinking a shaft was born. Thus, drilling for oil became the result of an idea born in the head of a not-too-well-educated

individual. Ironically, the financial backers sent Drake a telegram telling him to call off the search for oil on the same day that the first big oil strike was made!

Our second rule, then, is: *Do not allow your imagination to be stifled by negative thoughts or unfavorable influences from your environment.*

THE CREATIVE ORGANIZATION

If, after all of the above information has failed to move you, and you still insist that you're not an "idea person," then there is still a mission for you. As an executive, be aware that your organization must have creative talent if it is to survive. This means two things: hiring creative people to work for you becomes a necessity, and your responsibility in creating an atmosphere that is conducive to creativity is also quite important. This means that you must recognize and encourage creative talent within your organization. If you feel that you cannot or will not be an originator, then become a developer—it will pay off just as handsomely. In fact, presiding over a creative organization is, in itself, a creative act!

How can you recognize and encourage creative talent? According to the Johnson-O'Connor Foundation, the creative person is one who is capable of producing a multitude of new ideas in rapid succession. They call this trait "ideaphoria." Gary Steiner has a fairly exhaustive list of traits as follow:

The Creative Individual:

Conceptual fluency ... is able to produce a large number of ideas quickly.
Originality ... generates unusual ideas.
Separates source from content in evaluating information ... is motivated by interest in problem ... follows wherever it leads.

Suspends judgment ... avoids early commitment ... spends more time in analysis, exploration.

Less authoritarian ... has relativistic view of life.

Accepts own impulses ... playful undisciplined exploration.

Independence of judgment, less conformity, deviant, sees self as different.

Rich, "bizarre" fantasy life *and* superior reality orientation; controls.[7]

Organizations, as well, are responsible for providing a creative environment. Since creativity and organizational survival are two sides of the same coin, it becomes the responsibility of management to see to it that an atmosphere of creativity prevails as much of the time as possible. Again, Gary Steiner has outlined for us the salient features of the creative organization:

The Creative Organization:

Has idea men and women.

Open Channels of Communication.

Suggestion Systems.

Brain-storming.

Idea Units absolved of other responsibilities (R & D).

Encourages contact with outside sources (professional associations, convention, etc.).

Heterogeneous Personnel Policy (No straight-jacketed or rigid standards for personnel hiring).

Includes marginal, unusual types of people.

Assigns non-specialists to problems (they can sometimes see things that specialists cannot).

Allows eccentricity.

Has an objective, fact-founded approach.

Ideas evaluated on their merits, not on the status of the originator.

Invests in basic research; flexible, long-range planning.

Experiments with new ideas rather than prejudging on "rational" grounds; everything gets a chance.

More decentralization; diversified.

Administrative slack; time and resources to absorb errors (allowance for trial and error).

Risk-taking ethos ... tolerates and expects to take chances.

Not run as "tight ship."

Employees have fun (enjoy their work and their working environment).

Allows freedom to choose and pursue problems.

Freedom to discuss ideas.

Organizationally autonomous (analagous to decentralization).

Original and different objectives, not trying to be another "X".

Security of routine . . . allows innovation . . . "phillistines" provide stable, secure environment that allows "creators" to roam (at their pleasure).

Has separate units or occasions for generating vs. evaluating ideas. . . . separates creative from productive functions.[8]

Most successful organizations are open-minded to change; they understand the great value in having innovative, creative people around, and are sympathetic with the need for providing the kind of atmosphere in which creative imaginations can flourish. There are, of course, a few short-sighted organizations that feel that they can go on doing the same things forever. These organizations are doomed to failure, because they do not understand the basic nature of change. Our third rule, then, is: *Organizations must be creative in order to survive. It is the responsibility of the executives of the organization to see to it that a favorable creative environment is encouraged and maintained as much as possible.*

ONCE UPON A TIME . . .

The creative organization is nothing new. There are interesting examples from history in this century that can teach us a great deal about what creativity is. Let's look at a few examples.

Burma-Shave

Long before Madison Avenue was a household synonym for advertising expertise, Burma-Shave was being marketed and advertised in a way that would turn one of those Madison Avenue moguls green with envy. It all began in

1925 in Red Wing, Minnesota. Leonard Odell's grandfather was a lawyer who manufactured liniment on the side. Odell was an excellent salesman, but wasn't doing much with the liniment. Men were still shaving with brushes, and carrying them in their suitcases while traveling was a messy, smelly business (the brushes would turn green with mildew.) Odell hit on the idea of a brushless shaving cream. He got a chemist friend to come up with a formula that wasn't very good, but it gave them a start. Odell packaged the shaving cream in jars, and tried to sell them to local drug stores, without much success. He advertised them with a money-back guarantee, but still without much interest. They had improved the formula after 300 tries, and the product now was rather good. They were also almost dead broke. Then one day, Odell's brother Allan had an experience that changed their fortunes.

> Jars on Approval—if you want to starve to death fast, that's the way to do it. I guess Al was pretty discouraged. One day on the road between Aurora and Joliet he saw a small set of serial signs advertising a gas station: Gas, Oil, Restrooms, things like that—maybe a dozen of them—and then at the end a sign would point in to the gas station. Al Thought, "every time I see one of these setups, I read every one of the signs. So why can't you sell a product that way?[9]

They took their last capital—$200 and began to paint signs that could be placed along the roadside. The year 1925 was, coincidentally, just the time when automobiles were being produced that could travel long distances on newly constructed two-lane asphalt highways. Speeds were still at 40 miles per hour, so passing cars would be able to read the signs. The first signs were not the rhymed jingles that Burma-Shave became famous for, and a great deal of experimentation was yet to come. But the basic idea of stringing out five or six small signs along the side of the road was the beginning of a great success story. They set up a sign shop in 1926 and began to stencil their jingles. Below are a few examples (each line was a separate sign):[10]

Said Juliet
To Romeo
If You
Won't Shave
Go Homeo
Burma-Shave

He Married Grace
With Scratchy Face
He Only
Got One Day
Of Grace!
Burma-Shave

Put Your Brush
On The Shelf
The Darn Thing
Needs A
Shave Itself
Burma-Shave

With Glamor Girls
You'll Never Click
Bewhiskered
Like A Bolshevik
Burma-Shave

She Kissed
The Hairbrush
By Mistake
She Thought It Was
Her Husband Jake
Burma-Shave

'Mid Rising Taxes
Soaring Rents
Still Half a Pound
For Fifty Cents
Burma-Shave

The Burma-Shave jingles caught on well—so well in fact that there were over 35,000 sets of signs displayed along the highways in most states from Maine to Texas. Reading them became a national pasttime, and passengers in the car would vie for the privilege of reading them as they passed the signs. The Odells would rent space for the signs from farmers, and had regular crews to plant the signs and keep them repaired.

Of course, the Odells began to run out of jingles, so to keep their creativity running in high gear, they offered $100 for every jingle sent in by the public that was accepted. Reading those jingles and deciding on which ones to use was quite a chore in itself. The Burma-Shave Company also decided to use some of their advertising space for public service messages as well. Here are a few examples.[11]

Maybe You Can't
Shoulder a Gun
But You Can Shoulder
The Cost Of One
Buy Defense Bonds
Burma-Shave

You Can Beat
A Mile a Minute
But There Ain't
No Future
In It
Burma-Shave

Car In Ditch
Driver In Tree
Moon Was Full
So Was He
Burma-Shave

The interesting thing to bear in mind is that professional advertising men in Chicago thought the idea of roadside jingles worthless when Leonard Odell consulted them back in 1925. Burma-Shave signs continued to appear along the roadsides of America until the company was sold to Phillip Morris in 1963. During World War II, G.I.s all over the world put up their own Burma-Shave signs as a bit of nostalgic Americana. One group even put up Burma-Shave signs in the Antartic! Changing conditions, high-speed roadways and cars, and the high cost as well as the prohibition of billboard advertising, spelled the demise of the Burma-Shave signs. Once in a great while, they can still be spotted on rural roads that used to be the main highways, but they have practically disappeared now. Creative energy turned the Burma-Vita Company from a near disaster to a $3,000,000 gold mine in annual sales at its height, and taught a few lessons that Madison Avenue won't forget. In fact, they honored the company with a dinner in New York after Philip Morris took over. No one really knows where creative energy comes from; but in the case of Burma-Shave it was born out of sheer desperation and defeat. Perhaps these are the greatest motivators of all.

Just 100 Days

Franklin Delano Roosevelt became President on March 4, 1933. Most historians today are agreed that in just 100 days, from March 16 to June 16, during a special session of Congress, the groundwork of a revolutionary change in American domestic policy was laid. Roosevelt, it is interesting to note, came into the Presidency with no preconceived notions as to what road the country should take. He was a conservative, but knew that drastic measures of reform had to be taken if the United States was to avoid going down the road of militaristic fascism or communism that other countries were taking to solve their problems.

Accordingly, even before his inauguration, Roosevelt began to gather some of the best and brightest talent in the country to help develop the policies that would revive a sick and dying nation. Raymond Moley of Columbia University was given the task of recruiting some of the most able minds; he recruited such notables as Rexford Tugwell, Adolph Berle, Felix Frankfurter, Thomas Corcoran, and Benjamin Cohen. Together, these men, who were protéges of Roosevelt, made up what the newspapers quickly coined as "The Brains Trust," and the name stuck. These men quickly grouped and began making suggestions as to what kinds of policies and legislation should be introduced into a special session of Congress (the 73rd) that Roosevelt had called for the purpose of reforming the economic and social policies of the United States.

During this period, Roosevelt spoke with leaders from all over America, from every walk of life; he listened patiently to every proposal, never tiring, always seeking. He was, in short, the epitome of the creative leader who, in his search for a solution to the country's ills, left no stone unturned. Ultimately, the profoundly revolutionary legislative program that emerged (some of it was later declared unconstitutional by the Supreme Court) was not the product of one mind, but rather the product of a large number of bright people who were given free reign to be creative, to come up with the answers. Congress also drafted much of its own legislation, with a definitely creative flair. Thus in 100 days, a mind-boggling list of legislation was passed and America would never be the same again. A few are listed below:

Federal Emergency Relief Act
Agricultural Adjustment Act
Civilian Conservation Corps
National Industrial Recovery Act
Tennessee Valley Authority
Banking Reforms

Most important of all, however, was the fact that a group of highly creative people with little political experience was recruited to help solve the nation's problems. As Raymond Moley later described it, the fundamentally creative challenge was to rebuild the confidence of the American people:

Underneath all was a determination to achieve a psychological effect upon the country by the appearance of "action on many fronts." Roosevelt believed that the very quantity of legislation passed would inspire wonder and confidence.[12]

No doubt about it—Franklin Delano Roosevelt was a creative genius. He knew what would turn the American people on and restore their confidence. He knew *that* was the real problem. Roosevelt's uncanny shrewdness steered him toward creative people because he knew he needed a huge quantity of ideas of all kinds (grist for his mill) if he was going to succeed. One hundred days—and plenty of imagination—is all it took to change a nation.

A View From The Inside

Bell and Howell was one of the smaller companies struggling to retain a small share of the movie camera market—5 or 10 percent. During the 1960s the challenge that they had to face was how to retain their share of the market on a small budget? Peter G. Peterson, who was then president, pointed out:

One of the objectives ... is how to make a *unique* impression with a limited number of dollars. The second thing that occurs to us ... is that we cannot possibly hope with our limited funds to reach everyone; therefore, we keep asking ourselves: Is there a way we can effectively reach a certain segment of the market?[13]

As Peterson tells it, then, the challenge was how to do much with little; innovation certainly had to be the only bridge to success for this struggling company. One idea that struck Peterson came to him quite by accident. One Saturday morning, his young son turned on the television set, and there appeared a most intriguing program, "The Face of Red China." Peterson thought it was a pity that such a program had to be lost to the general public, and the idea occurred to him that Bell and Howell could do a lot for its image if it were to sponsor prime time public service programs. His idea ran contrary to the accepted thinking of the time—that you can only sell products on programs that entertain. In fact, controversial programs will probably be the death knell of your company went the arguments of those who thought they knew it all. The company went ahead with its sponsorship of controversial programs, and not only did they receive warm letters of approval from the public but also received a warm reception for their product line as well.

On another occasion, a friend came in with the idea that Bell and Howell might consider selling a camera outfit by direct mail. Most of the executives thought the idea was preposterous. One does not sell an expensive ($150) item through the mail. The customers have to have a chance to see it, to compare models before they buy, etc. Peterson found that they could experiment and try the idea for $10,-000, and they took the plunge. The result?

> If you were to show this direct-mail piece to a hundred marketing experts, nine out of ten would tell you that it is preposterous; it just will not work. Here is an outfit of movie equipment that sells for $150, and all it says is: Shoot the show; get a couple of rolls of film free; if you don't like it, send it back; if you do like it, 24 months to pay, and an attractive combination of lights. The startling thing is that this one method of selling has been extremely successful and is now a basis of important new business at Bell & Howell, in which we have set up a subsidiary devoted exclusively to selling by direct mail.[14]

On another occasion, Peterson was becoming increasingly concerned over the escalating cost of rebates to Bell and Howell dealers. Then, one day at lunch, the price of the company's stock came up, and the single word, "stock" struck Peterson like a thunderclap.

Now why has no one ever thought of that before? Why not make dealers stockholders in Bell & Howell? Instead of giving them money, which doesn't achieve anything, why don't we make them stockholders and build a longer-term relationship? We have done this for two or three years now, and we are finding that, at about a third of the cost of cash incentives, we are able to achieve a much more permanent effect and a much deeper impact.[15]

Bell and Howell never really became one of the giants of the industry, but that's not the point. The interesting thing for us to observe is that their creative managers were willing to experiment, to innovate, and to tread on ground that the "professionals" thought was dangerous, and the results proved to be most gratifying indeed.

What's Your I.Q.?

Your I.Q. (imagination quotient) will prove to be a very important factor in your life as an executive. Being a creative executive can, at times, be a painful experience. It may mean sticking your neck out, taking an unpopular, or what even may seem to be a ridiculous stand. But in the long run, you'll have achieved enormous satisfaction. You'll have made something from nothing (just an idea), and you'll have made a new world in the process. Listed below are some guidelines that you should keep in mind. These will help you to be a more creative executive.

1. Do you make suggestions freely? Are you willing to work out suggestions for improvements and pass them along to your superiors, even if they seem to pay no attention to the suggestions? Don't become discouraged. It could be that suggestion 99 will be the one that will be a bonanza.

2. Do you encourage those working under you to develop new ideas? Are you patient with them when they present their new ideas to you? Solicitation of ideas is the mark of a creative executive.

3. Do you keep track of your ideas? Do you write down your ideas in a notebook?

4. Do you follow through an idea, even though it may seem to hold little possibility? It is important that an idea be followed through to the end. Perhaps it is not useful now, but what is learned in the meantime can be valuable later on.

5. Do you track your ideas and follow them with enthusiasm and with a feeling of great expectations? Remember, enthusiasm is contagious. When those around you see your spirit, they are quite likely to become infected by your enthusiasm. Psychological studies have shown that group achievement is at its highest pitch when there is enthusiasm for the project at hand.

6. Are you receptive to all ideas? Do not throw out ideas because at first blush they appear to be silly, preposterous, or unworkable. More important, don't do that to ideas that are advanced to you by your colleagues or subordinates. Remember: *Every idea is worth consideration!*

7. Do you persevere? Solutions are sometimes very elusive. How much you persevere can have a direct relationship to the amount of creative problem solving you can do.

8. Do you tackle problems in which there is little interest shown by others in your organization? This can sometimes prove to be rewarding. For example, preparing a contingency plan when there seems to be no need for one can really raise your stock when the need suddenly arises.

9. Do you encourage collective creativity? Do you ever get your subordinates together in an atmosphere where brainstorming can take place?

10. Do you think that you are creative? If your answer is no, try to tackle some difficult problems, and I

think you'll find that you have changed your mind. Frequently, lack of creativity is either fear or laziness, nothing more. You should now take steps to improve your I.Q., and begin putting those good ideas to work.

SUMMARY

Imagination and the ability to use and develop it is responsible for the development of modern industrial civilization. Imagination is also what separates the free enterprise societies from the socialist societies. The individual who feels that he or she cannot be creative is badly mistaken. Studies have shown that everyone has creative ability. Creative ability has to be exercised to be an asset, however.

There are several steps to developing your creative imagination. The first and most important step is to be motivated. Without motivation, nothing will happen. The other five steps to problem solving are: fluency by bombardment with ideas, gestation, deliberation, suspended judgment and testing, and solution. All of the steps in problem solving in a creative way must involve a serious and profound study of all of the factors surrounding the problem to be solved.

There are roadblocks that will hamper our creativity, if we allow them to. Among these are: too much logic, rigidity, timidity, and self-discouragement.

For those who still feel that they are not creative people, there is an important task to be performed. That is, they must see to it that the kind of environment exists in their organizations that will promote creative thinking as well as creative people, for that will probably be the ultimate salvation of your organization.

There are some interesting case studies drawn from the past that demonstrate that creative imagination is a necessary quality for any organization in any age. These case studies are Burma-Shave, the Franklin D. Roosevelt Administration (100 days), and the Bell and Howell Company.

Finally, it is important that you continue to improve and maintain your I.Q. (imagination quotient).

THE THREE RULES FOR DEVELOPING CREATIVE IMAGINATION

1. Anyone can be creative, provided that he or she is motivated, enthusiastic, and follows the five-step method of problem solving: fluency, gestation, deliberation, suspended judgment and testing, and solution.
2. Do not allow your imagination to be stifled by negative thoughts or unfavorable influences from your environment.
3. Organizations must be creative in order to survive. It is the responsibility of the executives of the organization to see to it that a favorable creative environment is encouraged and maintained as much as possible.

EXERCISES FOR CHAPTER 8

1. Conduct a brainstorming session. Give the group a problem and lay down the ground rules. Use three different kinds of topics:

   (a) How to improve a product. Use something simple such as a paper clip, a spoon, or a pencil.
   (b) How to improve a service. Use the sanitation service of your town or city or the fire department.
   (c) How to improve the structure of an organization.

   Keep a stopwatch and conduct the sessions around given periods of time (5 minutes; 10 minutes, etc.), and see how many ideas you get each time. Try the experiment a few times, and see if the rate of production does not increase with each successive session.

2. How many suggestions for improving, beautifying, making more pleasant, and more efficient can you come up with at your place of work?

3. Pretend that you are an advertising copywriter. Write an ad that will extol the virtues of your client's new disposable diapers.

4. Pretend that you are going to run for political office. Write some political speeches that will tell the public why they should vote for you.

NOTES

1. "Innovation: Has America Lost its Edge?", in Newsweek, June 4, 1979.

2. Alex F. Osborn, *Applied Imagination*. Charles Scribner's Sons, New York, 1963. p. 69.

3. Richard McKeon (ed), *The Basic Works of Aristotle*. Random House, New York, 1941. p. 587.

4. Mrs. Paget Toynbee, (ed), *The Letters of Horace Walpole*, Clarendon Press, Oxford, 1903, v. iii. pp. 203–204.

5. A very good short introduction to meditation and relaxation is *The Relaxation Response* by Herbert Benson, M.D., William Morrow and Co., New York, 1975.

6. Eugene K. Von Fange, *Professional Creativity*, Prentice-Hall, Englewood Cliffs, N.J., 1959, p. 45. Quoted from Scott Nicholson, "Group Creative Thinking," *Management Record*, July 1956.

7. Gary Steiner (ed), *The Creative Organization*. University of Chicago Press, Chicago, 1965. pp. 16–18.

8. Gary Steiner, Ibid.

9. Frank Rowsome, Jr., *The Verse by the Side of The Road*, Stephen Green Press, Brattleboro, Vt., 1978, pp. 13–14.

10. Ibid.

11. Ibid.

12. Raymond Moley, *The First New Deal.* Harcourt, Brace & World, New York, 1966. p. 339.

13. Gary Steiner, op. cit., p. 186.

14. Ibid, pp. 188–189.

15. Ibid, pp. 189–190.

9

Now!

It's Moving Time

Whether you are going to seek a managerial position elsewhere or you are going to seek advancement within your own organization, there are a great many things that you can do to enhance your own opportunities. Some clues from the executive world have already begun to reach the general public. An interesting article in this regard appeared recently in *Fortune* magazine.[1] In the article, Herbert Meyer indicates that many corporate executives, intent on polishing their own images either for promotion or for better jobs elsewhere, are hiring consultants who specialize, for a handsome fee, in smoothing out the executive's rough edges, and presenting him or her as younger looking, sharper, wittier, etc. These consultants are called "image consultants" in the trade, and they charge handsome fees (upwards of $1,000 a month) for their services. Yet, the same services that they provide their clients with are also available to you at no cost because you can do the same things that those consultants do for their clients, if you develop a few strategies that you can use for yourself.

First of all, let's remember that "you can't make a silk purse out of a sow's ear." You cannot project an image that is so false that it fails to jibe with reality. But there are ways for you to enhance your appeal as well as your image, without straying too far from the real you. Let's look at what you can accomplish as your own image consultant.

Strategy One

Find out as much about the organization that you hope to work for as you can. Especially important in this regard is what traits or values it prizes most highly in its executives. For example, does this organization place greater emphasis on "team players" than on "loners?" Or the other way around? What kind of a public image does the organization have? How much can you find out about the values held by the top echelon of the organization? How much do you know about its products or services? What can you find out about the people who are middle level managers? Is there great turnover? Why? Before even considering a managerial job with an organization, you should become a fountain of information on that organization. You can do this in several ways: by consulting with people who have worked there before or are perhaps working there now. Sometimes there are discrete ways of doing this, without showing your hand. You can make inquiries within the industry (again, discretely), and you can make generous use of the library. There is much that can be learned about any organization that you are contemplating joining. The more informed you are about *their* problems, the better you'll be able to offer *yourself* as a good solution.

Strategy Two

Since the image makers concentrate on appearance as well as on ability, perhaps there's something to the idea that "clothes make the man or woman." Are you well groomed? Do you dress your role? Being overdressed is not the answer, but being dressed in a way that makes you look quietly successful and competent can make a strong impression. Generally, first impressions are most lasting of all. An initial impression that is poor can ruin your chances of being hired for a coveted executive position. Your appearance is certainly a clue to what's in the package. "Ah," but you may say, "I'm a diamond in the rough." That may be so, but prove that you are a diamond in the rough *after* you have shown what a valuable asset you are; otherwise, you may never have the chance. If you feel that you are not a good judge of how to dress, consult someone in whom you have confidence—a friend or relative, or even the store where you buy your clothes. Investing in a good appearance is well worth the cost.[2]

Strategy Three

Become a good communicator. Although we have already stressed the need for good communications within the organizational framework, there is a far greater need —that of being able to project and communicate with someone who is considering you for a job. Taking lessons in articulation and/or dramatics can also be a great asset. People who project well do so with all parts of their bodies: their eyes, speech, and gestures. Although you can help yourself greatly by using a tape recorder and a mirror, or even practicing with a friend, it might be wise to attend institutes like those run by the Dale Carnegie organization. Although they are expensive, they are worthwhile because you'll find yourself in a setting where you'll be forced to communicate. The corporate image-makers that we discussed earlier place heavy stress on this ability to communicate effectively, so there must be something to it. Moreover, it is quite surprising how many top-notch executives are really so poor at communicating their thoughts to others via the spoken word. Many corporations today are giving their executives lessons in speech making for just that purpose. There is another important reason why your ability to articulate your ideas is more necessary than ever. Today's executive has to be a spokesman to the world outside of his organization's door. He or she has to be a spokesperson to the world at large, the stockholders, the press, the Congress, the government, etc. An executive who cannot communicate well, therefore, can be an albatross around the neck of his organization, and no one wants that.

Strategy Four

Executives, like academicians, are increasingly finding themselves in a "publish or perish" situation. Some are even going so far as to have articles for business or trade publications ghost-written for them. While it is not necessary for you to go to those lengths, you should, however, embark on a do-it-yourself program as soon as you can. How? It's really simple. Most newspapers have columns that solicit editorials and comments from the public. Many television stations have "speak out" programs or other public access programs. Many industry trade papers and magazines will welcome articles from executives. They do not even have to be well-written; the editor can take care of that. The point is that you'll soon find your name becoming well-known in your industry. A solid reputation as an authority can thus be acquired. A friend of mine who is an attorney began to write articles for the *Lawyers' Weekly Report.* After a few articles had appeared, he was amazed to find how many fellow barristers and even judges began to know him by name, and regard his as an attorney who is at least a minor authority. Writing an article can be a great asset to your career. It makes you a kind of authority, and its importance cannot be underestimated. Even if you don't write well, try it. All you need is the specialized knowledge or opinions that you want to impart to others.

Strategy Five

Because organizations are increasingly concerned about their public image in an age where consumers and the general public are usually in a posture of anger and dissent, the involvement of their executives in some kind of community service work has taken on greatly increased significance. Many executives, therefore, have become deeply involved in community activities. They have not only enhanced their own images; they have improved the images of their parent organizations as well. Membership in public organizations, in addition to making you feel that you have done something for your fellow man, also will enable you to broaden your contacts by meeting other executives from other organizations who are similarly engaged in community service work. A busy executive, however, may find public service work burdensome. Time spent away from his or her family may cause increased resentment. The best way to continue this kind of public work, and still maintain a happy family life, is to involve the members of your family in your activities. Not only should you be a service volunteer, but enlist your spouse and your children as well. That way, it will be a rewarding experience for all and will keep the family together. At any rate, community service in the Red Cross, the Boy Scouts, etc. is an excellent way to demonstrate that you can represent your organization effectively to the outside world.

SHOW AND TELL

From the time that we are children in kindergarten, we are encouraged to "show and tell" about things we have accomplished or that are important in our lives. In a sense, we are already giving interviews. But now, life is becoming more complicated, and we are earnestly involved in the adult version of show and tell—having an interview for a job.

What is the unique chemistry that makes the interviewer receptive to you instead of someone else? Put in other terms, how can you make the interview that you're going to have result in an executive job offer? The interview itself will be the crucial moment in culmination of your job search. After you have been selected as one of five finalists, for example, you are now ready for the interview or what is probably closer to reality, a series of interviews. What produces a good interview; conversely, what are the pitfalls? Remember, when an employer is looking at you, he's really seeing dollar signs, efficiency reports, problems being solved, etc. You represent to your interviewer the answer to at least some of his problems. So he's not about to hire someone who will plunge him deeper into chaos. He needs, instead, someone who will improve *his*—and the organization's—position. It's not just you sitting across the desk from the vice president. It's what you represent that is most meaningful. Let's take a look at which characteristics and which kinds of chemistry seem to come closest to a good interview. There are six elements that will provide the basis for a successful interview. Remember, however, that you wouldn't be undergoing an interview at all if the organization weren't seriously interested in your services. You have already gone through a series of paper eliminations. Perhaps you are one of five finalists out of a hundred that were originally considered. Now the problem is how to become the final finalist!

The first element in your interview will be that of *poise*. This not only includes good appearance, it also includes good manners. A certain amount of enlightened deference to your interviewer is necessary here. Pay attention to the social amenities. Do not appear to be overbearing. Although an important interview is an occasion to make anyone nervous, try not to do such things as fidgeting (keep your hands folded), smoking, (plenty of time for that later —smoking is a distraction, so refuse even if you are offered a cigarette), or other activities that will make you appear ill at ease. Remember, it's just the opposite effect that you are trying to communicate.

A second element is that of thoughtfulness. Jumping to answer a question makes you appear impulsive, especially when the question is of a controversial nature, and will give the impression that you "shoot from the hip." Unless that's the kind of organization that you're joining (chances are that it isn't), don't give that impression. You are being seriously considered precisely because you *are* a serious, thoughtful person, so there's no need to give the wrong impression. Instead, after being asked a question that was probably asked to reveal your values as well as your judgment, take the time to reflect or ponder before you give your answer. Right or wrong, it will make a much better impression if you appear thoughtful rather than simply a reactive type. Also, never be afraid to reveal your ignorance on a subject. It is dishonest to say you know something when you don't. You'll be respected much more if you simply say, "I don't know, but I can find out." Appearing to be dogmatic is definitely not the type of impression that you'll want to convey to an intelligent executive.

A third element is that of drive or ambition. Somehow, you must convey to your interviewer that you are a person who is endowed strongly with goal-oriented behavior. How can this be accomplished? For one thing, giving the impression that you are in good condition, physically, that you are energetic, and that you are constantly searching for new ideas and new methods are good topics to start with. For another, giving the impression that you really enjoy a challenge for its own sake; that you place a high value on such things as achievement, growth, and recognition, are also valuable assets in your quest for a position of leadership. Money is important, but it will come along with achievement and recognition, so stress those values that are most important first, and then talk about money last. Drive and ambition are not tied strictly to money alone. They are tied in with other values as well, and although the salary that you can expect to receive is certainly a legitimate topic of discussion, you are considering the job for many other more challenging reasons than money.

A fourth element in the successful interview is a rather elusive quality that we can call sparkle, wit, or humor. We all should be endowed with a sense of humor; it's an essential quality for an executive to have. While you're not being considered for your social talents alone, they do comprise part of the total picture of you as a person, and can give you a comparative edge during the competition for an executive position. Do not misunderstand. You're not expected to be a bon vivant or comedian; you're much too serious a person for that. But you can still be serious and be a good, witty conversationalist. This may be a difficult characteristic for you to develop, but lots of good reading and developing as broad and varied a circle of friends as possible will be a great asset in developing your conversational skills. A varied program of reading will also help a great deal in this regard, because if all else fails, you can bring up some facts or ideas from your reading that will enliven the dialogue considerably.

The fifth element is your leadership potential. After all, you are being considered for a position of leadership. What kind of leader will you be? Some clues to this are seen in the way in which you radiate confidence and a positive attitude. It may be hackneyed and reminiscent of Horatio Alger, but some of the old techniques are still valid. Nothing will ever replace a firm handshake, a warm, reassuring smile, good posture and bearing, and looking the other person in the eye. All of these gestures imply an openness that are bound to be well-received as signs of self-confidence, and that in turn is a sure sign of the ability to lead. As your interviewers will be constantly sizing you up for your leadership potential, it becomes important that you give every indication possible of that potential. One who feels at ease with himself or herself and has a good self-image is bound to radiate that kind of confidence.

Finally, the sixth element in an interview is to come across as a positive thinker. A person who thinks negatively will come across that way in an interview; he will not be able to help himself. So putting yourself into a positive and optimistic frame of mind will do wonders for your interview as well as for your spirit. This includes a cheerful outlook on life in general, and not being the Doomsday Dan that we discussed in Chapter 1. Behaving like an optimist may not be easy, especially when your interviewer is in a deeply pessimistic mood, but if you can come across positively, your optimism and cheerful mood will be most welcome.

In any interview, avoid different kinds of hostility. Hostility can be veiled like other feelings, but the vibrations will come across as surely as though you were openly hostile. Why would you be hostile anyway? Perhaps you're feeling frustrated, perhaps the interviewer is asking questions or making statements that upset you, or perhaps you feel that you're not really in the running and that they are just playing cat-and-mouse with you. Whatever the reasons, don't allow yourself to be conquered by fear and anger. These emotions will not allow the real you—the optimistic, friendly and confident leader—to emerge.

Finally, it is always a good idea to follow up any interview with a letter of appreciation. You never know what may happen in the future, and letters of appreciation are always well-remembered. It may also be an excellent idea to write down your reaction to the interview while it is still fresh in your mind. Such an analysis will be helpful to you in later interviews. If you feel that you made any mistakes, a review is the best possible way for you to see those mistakes and take appropriate remedial action. Our first rule, then, is: *Your search for an executive position will involve two important methods: strategy and tactics. Strategy means finding out as much about the organization, its values, methods, and management as you can. Tactics means that you have studied all of the circumstances of a successful interview.*

There is one other aspect to the successful search for an executive position. This aspect is your resume. So much has been written about successful resume preparation that to repeat it here would probably be irrelevant. There are, however, some good, basic rules that are worthwhile keeping in mind.

Rules for Resumes

1. Spend as much time and effort on your resume as you would on grooming yourself for an interview. It may be the only picture of you that a prospective employer will ever see.
2. Always have your resume professionally typed and printed. It is well worth the cost. Have the heading designed by an artist or a printer who designs stationery. Have your own personal stationery similarly designed. Have business cards made up. These are all marks of distinction and individuality. They are what will make you different, hence more attractive.
3. Your resume should tell your prospective employer what you can do to make conditions better for him. The only way this can be done is to tell him in your resume how you have improved conditions for your previous employers. Don't be afraid to blow your own horn, as long as you are truthful.
4. Don't mix in a lot of trivia or irrelevant information with material relating to your professional skills. If you want to include hobbies, marital status, etc., put those in an inconspicuous place. Put the material that will tell the reader of the resume what a great asset you'll be to the organization in the most prominent place where it counts!
5. Don't take chances with spelling, grammar, etc. If you're not very good at those things, have your resume done by a professional service. Mistakes on resumes or in letters generally make a very poor impression.
6. Update your resume every 6 months. Keep abreast of your achievements.

THE CLIMB FROM WITHIN

Let's assume that you have now secured that coveted executive job. You are still climbing up the steep road to the powerful position of Number One. Along the way there are many lessons to be learned and situations to be handled. There are three categories into which your relationships will fall. At this point it will be a good idea to consider each of these categories separately.

The first category is your relationship with your subordinates. How well you get along with those under your direction is an important determinant in how much more power you'll eventually be given within your organization. How well can you motivate your subordinates? Do you confront a person working under your direction with the accusation that he or she is not performing as expected? Or do you simply put off the confrontation hoping that the need for it will go away? Can you get the subordinates as enthusiastic as yourself over a project? Do you have an unusual amount of absenteeism? Is there much grumbling? All of these and many more questions are to be answered in determining what kind of a boss you are. How your subordinates perceive you and what they think of you will have a direct relationship to the kind of performance they'll turn in. Chances are, the better they perform, the higher your stock will rise in the organization, and the more powerful you'll become. With an increase in power, you'll be able to provide your division with increased benefits (or at least, the people who work under you will *think* that you can), and this will enhance your standing with your subordinates. Consequently, a great deal of the support that you'll receive from your people will depend to a great extent on how successfully you can exercise power within the organization.

Your responsibilities as a supervisor, therefore, need great care and attention. The first responsibility that you will have is to be supportive of your employees. Good supervision calls for an attitude that those who work under you can feel confident in. If the atmosphere is one of strained relations where fear and tension rule, then your subordinates are never really going to feel free to discuss problems, make suggestions that could be valuable, etc. Moreover, when a subordinate feels that he has contributed something more intrinsic to the job than just the outward motions, he will go home feeling good about it, and as we have already seen, a sense of achievement ranks very high on the employees' scale of values.

How you handle the employee who is not doing well on the job is also important to your career. It may sometimes take a great deal of discussion to get at the root of that person's problem. Patient investigation, however, will ultimately pay off for you. Frank discussion of the employee's feelings toward you, toward other employees, and toward his job will also result in improved work attitudes. Supervision requires tremendous amounts of patience. I once had a boss who used to moan, "If only people would stop behaving like people!" They're not going to, and you're going to find yourself in the middle of controversial backbiting, jealousy, and hostility between your employees much of the time. The principal way to overcome these kinds of problems is to have the employees identify with your goals as well as with the goals of the organization. Once the goals of the organization are in harmony with those of the employees, there will be increased cooperation and less tension. "That," you may say, "is easier said than done." True, but it is possible. A number of strategies are available here if we will but use them.

One strategy is to share information with your employees. Let them know how well the organization is doing, or conversely, how poorly. It makes no difference if the news is good or bad. In fact, bad news frequently spurs people on to more productivity, as long as there is hope for recovery. Sharing information is not the same as sharing decisions—it's important to keep that in mind. In a larger setting, a newsletter to employees can be a great asset. If there are new goals or even new developments that can be shared with the employee who is the lowest on the ladder, so much the better.

Another strategy is to throw a challenge to the subordinates. Put in the form of a problem, they can be asked either collectively or singly to contribute their advice and wisdom to the solution of problems. While they may contribute nothing of value to the resolution of the problem, they will at least come away with more highly polished egos, and that can be worth a lot in productivity.

A third strategy is to conduct open meetings with groups of employees. If you use this strategy, be sure that it's a "meeting" and not a "party." Creating an informal, sociable climate to relax the atmosphere is very destructive and will relax nothing at all. In fact, it may cause people to say things that they'll regret later on. A formal meeting with no diversions, however, can be an excellent way of determining employee attitudes. People should be encouraged to be as frank and as candid with each other as possible, but to keep personality differences on a very low profile. Group meetings can quickly degenerate into group therapy if you allow the goals of the organization to slip away from you.

Effective supervision means that you communicate well with your subordinates, i.e., you give them clear, understandable directions; you communicate with them in such a way that there is no room left for doubt as to what you meant; and you encourage them to ask questions if they are in doubt. When people understand their jobs and understand what is expected of them, productivity and efficiency climb.

Finally, it is always important to remember that you are only as strong as the weakest link in your chain. Many a leader has been defeated by his own unhappy crew and subsequently lost his position of leadership. If your employees see you as unfair, excessively authoritarian, or capricious, they will retaliate, rest assured. Absenteeism, stealing, loafing on the job, noncompliance, and carelessness are ways in which employees get even, and it can cost you your job. So, remember—power is a trust. Handle it carefully.

A second category is that of peer relationships. Climbing the organizational ladder has most often been described in such unflattering terms as "the rat race." To be sure, the struggle for dominance in an organization is going to be highly competitive. Anytime that there is money and power at stake, there'll be plenty of competition. But there are also strategies that will help you to avoid some of the worst features of that rat race. Bear in mind that all organizations have politics. By definition, politics is the art of living with each other, and nowhere can that be more true than with your peers in the organization. But as I suggested at the beginning of this book, don't let the politics of the organization turn you into a Machiavellian; instead, fight for your position in a constructive manner— you'll be glad that you did. What, then, are some of the strategies that we can use in getting along well with our peers, while at the same time making progress toward the top?

Playing the game of politics within the organization means that you must have access to as much information as possible. One way to do this is to build a network of friends or allies who will be able to feed you the information that you need to have. Much of this information is "grapevine" quality, hence is not general knowledge. So having your own intelligence network is quite important. If you get information from your peers, you'll probably be expected to trade information so as to build *their* intelligence network as well. If you get along well with those peers, it probably is a good idea to trade off information, but you can be selective about what you trade. Even though your peers are competitors with you for that leadership position, there has to be some cooperation or the organization will fall apart.

Another strategy is that of building alliances with your peers. The "you scratch my back and I'll scratch yours" brand of politics is frequently successful. As long as you and your competition are not after the same thing, you can afford to be allies with each other in the quest for mutual survival. For example, seeking to enlist the aid of the manager of another department to help you get extra office help might ultimately require that you later help him in acquiring extra office space.

Informal get togethers with peers are also a good method of achievement. In a friendly atmosphere, much can be learned in a sociable setting. Sharing information implies trust and it is important to remember that if a peer says uncomplimentary things about the boss, or the other executives, don't use it against him. On the other hand, by being a good listener and by always asking for advice and showing appreciation for it, you will soon find that you have enlisted many allies. Frequently, intelligence can come to you via one of your subordinates. Having good rapport with the people who work under you can pay off handsomely in broadening your network of information.

Another suggestion is that you attempt to bring yourself under the wing of an executive who has been in the organization for a long time. Having him take an interest in your future can mean that he will teach you a lot about the organization as well as your job. Moreover, that senior executive is perhaps getting close to retirement, so he will have no particular axe to grind.

The politics of an organization are going to be competitive, so competitive that it will be difficult to bear the backbiting and scheming for position. The game has to be played, it is true; but you can keep it on a high level. Remember the old Russian proverb, "He who lies down with dogs, gets up with fleas." I think you will find that being competent, candid, and honest will pay good dividends in the long run. So play the game, but play it on your terms, not on theirs.

The third category is that of relations with your boss. Obviously, how well you do in the organization will depend heavily on your boss's attitude toward you; and his attitude toward you will be largely conditioned by your feelings about him. So how you perceive your boss is an important factor. Do you trust him? Can you depend on his word? Does he say one thing and do another or is he always consistent? Is he open-minded to suggestions? Does he give praise generously? Or is he more generous with criticism? Does he delegate authority well? How is your boss perceived by others in the organization? Does he need to have his ego massaged much of the time? Does he identify well with the goals of your organization? These are but a few of the questions that you have to answer if you're going to deal with your boss effectively. At the same time that you are manager of a department, you are subordinate to someone else, so your relationship to your boss is important, if you are to achieve the goals that you have set for yourself.

Your first strategy, of course, is to please your boss. There is a dual relationship of dependency and autonomy that is curiously intertwined. Leavitt comments:

> Partly to protect their relationships with their own superiors and partly on rational grounds, superiors tend to demand that subordinates objectively justify their actions, often in advance of the actions themselves. The superior expects his subordinates to be "businesslike" in their methods as well as their results. This requirement may force people's dependency underground, so they act more and more independently, though they really would like a shoulder to weep on.[3]

The subordinate, in other words, is caught in a bind. He or she wants to do a good job and wants to protect the boss, yet finds himself frequently "protecting" the boss by giving him selective facts and data that he would like to see, rather than that which he should see. This might be an excellent idea, as long as things go swimmingly, but unfortunately, they do not. So you cannot really please your boss by distorting reality, as tempting as it may seem, because *your* reality is the actions that your boss expects you to take as well as the manner (style) in which you take those actions. Yet, many subordinates, operating more as a result of fear than of rationality, are guilty of misleading their superiors and can cause real damage. So your first strategy is to please your boss by giving him the truth. Sometimes it hurts; it's rarely pleasant. Sometimes it may be a bad reflection on you; admitting mistakes is unpleasant. In the long run, however, your strategy will pay off, because your superior will know that he can trust you, and that there will never be any cause to doubt the facts that you give him.

A second strategy follows from the first. If your superior trusts you, he will delegate more authority to you. That puts you in a position to begin making suggestions for change. It is an ego problem for many superiors that causes them to think the way they have done things has been for the best, and making a suggestion to the boss that perhaps there is a *better* way is attacking his ego. Instead, why not slowly spoon-feed him reasons why certain changes would be better, and at the same time convince him that you are suggesting these chages for *his* benefit; that these changes will make him look better in the eyes of *his* superiors.

A third strategy is that of loyalty. Loyalty is another one of those concepts that are "old-fashioned," but it's still very much in style. Demonstrating that you are loyal, and that you are looking out for your superior's best interests is not always easy. In fact, there'll be times when conflict will be erupting between your loyalty to your organization and your loyalty to your boss. What should you do? If the conflict involves your loyalty to the goals or objectives of your organization, you should be loyal to those objectives first. If this conflict will cause harm to the organization, then it should be resolved in the organization's favor, and you should attempt to make it clear to your boss why you feel that his conflict with the organization's goals are a serious hindrance to him and to you. He will probably be grateful in the long run. Of course, conditions and the complexity of organizational life are not always so crystal clear that we can see any conflicts in goals, beliefs, etc; that is why old-fashioned loyalty becomes such a valuable asset. Ideally, there should never be a real conflict between loyalty to one's boss and loyalty to the organization. McClelland and Burnham write:

> Managers motivated by personal power are not disciplined enough to be good institution builders, and often their subordinates are loyal to them as individuals rather than to the institution that they both serve. When a personal-power manager leaves, disorganization often follows. His subordinates' strong group spirit which the manager has personally inspired, deflates. The subordinates do not know what to do for themselves.[4]

McClelland and Burnham go on to point out that the "institutional" manager, one who identifies first with the goals of the organization, makes life a lot easier for the subordinates, because he does not demand personal loyalty at the cost of the organization. So a strategy of loyalty to one's superiors is a good idea, but be careful never to allow it to get out of hand to the point that it can threaten the well-being of the organization. A good example of the conflict in loyalty felt by a subordinate might be the following:

> Jack Price is vice president in charge of sales for an already established product that has been a steady seller for the corporation for the past 10 years. The corporate leadership wants to set up a new division that will produce a new series of products that, if successful, will probably eclipse Jack Price's division. Jack Price is determined to use all of his influence to sabotage the new division, because he sees it as a threat to his job. Al Snow, Price's assistant, feels that he should tell the corporate leadership about Price's plan to sabotage the new division before it can make any headway.

In this example, Al Snow, Price's assistant, should place loyalty to the organization and its goals above loyalty to his boss, who is acting selfishly and in a very short-sighted manner. Loyalty is important, but when a leader demands personal loyalty, unless he is the absolute king of the organization, it is a wise idea indeed to think about where your real obligation lies.

Last, a fourth strategy is that of making your boss your mentor. You can learn a great deal from your superiors, and if you show appreciation and encourage them to teach you what they know, you will learn even more. There really is no substitute for experience, and there probably never will be. You will probably find that your boss will not only be flattered, but will be eager to pass on his wealth of experience to you. When General Douglas MacArthur retired, he made a poignant speech to Congress, and reiterated an old barracks room ballad: "Old Soldiers Never Die . . . They Just Fade Away." In a way, that is what happens to managers too. Most managers would like to believe that

they have left a little bit of themselves with the organization that they have struggled to help build for so many
years. If they are proud of what they have done, they'll be
more than eager to share their past with you. Your boss-
mentor was once "wet behind the ears, too," and he is
human like you. Your support and loyalty will be well-
rewarded with a wealth of insights.

Our second rule, then is: *In your climb to the top, you
will experience different kinds of relationships with three
different groups: subordinates, peers, and superiors. For
each group that you deal with there are different strategies as well as different relationships.*

MEASURE FOR MEASURE

As in any business, you should keep a running inventory
on yourself. Such an inventory should tell you where you
have been, what current achievements you have made,
and areas that need repair or improvement, or perhaps the
needed acquisition of new skills. You could even keep a
record on your social life as well, because social contacts
are going to be a definite part of your leadership role.

An inventory data sheet could be designed and maintained by you, similar to the example on page 243. The
sample inventory sheet is but an example of what you can
do. Design your own, and keep it year by year. This way,
you will be able to see what skills you have attained, and
what kinds of skills and development you still need.

Most people, executives included, will confide that they
are not in occupations that they had planned for. I once
met the district manager of a life insurance company who
confided that he was trained as a mechanical engineer. He
graduated during the Great Depression when there were
no engineering jobs to be had, so he joined the life insurance business and stayed in it, rising eventually to become
a district manager. Another man who was trained to be an
architect finally made a full-time career out of his hobby,
music, and established one of the few colleges in existence

Inventory for 1978–1979

Courses taken in last 5 years	Tax accounting Advanced computer science Management workshop Communications workshop Labor and management negotiations
Skills acquired in last 5 years	Advertising layout and copywriting Customer survey questionnaire design New product testing Use of E.D.P. equipment
Associations joined this past year	Junior Chamber of Commerce Community Council
Reading program this past year	How many books have you read? What kinds? Public affairs? Fiction? How well informed are you?
Achievement, recognition	Was given a $3,000 raise this year Promised a promotion
Travel	Do you travel in connection with your work? Where do you go on vacation?
Social contacts this past year	Have they increased or decreased? How many new people have you gotten friendly with? What kinds of professions do they have?
Business contacts this past year	What new business contacts have you made within your industry? At what levels? (Vice presidents?)
Relationships at work this past year	In your opinion, have they improved, gotten worse, or are they about the same as last year? Treat each group, subordinates, peers, and superiors, separately.
Any unique or unusual developments this past year	List here anything that may have happened that was new and unexpected, such as having new responsibilities added to your job description
My progress for the past year has been	Write your opinion of how much progress you have made towards your goal of leadership this past year.

I need to develop more skills and more depth in the following:
1. Data processing
2. Labor negotiations
3. Marketing

almost solely dedicated to contemporary music. It has become a huge success and has earned an international reputation.

The point is, that if you think you know exactly what you'll be doing 10 or 20 years from now, you're probably wrong. That's what makes life mysterious and interesting. It's also what makes it even more cogent that you keep some kind of running inventory on yourself. Review your accomplishments, your skills, and then try to determine areas that you are deficient in. Your next year's inventory should show that you have covered at least some of those deficiencies. We all need goals. An inventory is one good way of accomplishing them. Our third rule, then, is: *Develop and maintain an inventory, year by year, of your goals, skills, accomplishments, and deficiencies.*

Summary

A number of strategies are being adopted by today's executives, and these strategies can be adopted by you at little cost. These strategies include: Research on the organization that you are interested in joining, improving your appearance, becoming a good communicator, and becoming better known by a program of publications of letters to the editor, articles in trade magazines, etc. Other strategies include performing public service work in your community, and making yourself better known as a person who is interested in public affairs, because corporations are quite sensitive today to their public image.

A great deal of time and energy should be put into your preparation for interviews. Interviews mean that you have been selected as a finalist, and you should regard them as very important. There are a number of factors that, when put together, can account for a very successful interview. These factors include poise, thoughtfulness, drive, sparkle, leadership potential, positiveness, and the avoidance of hostility. Above all, you must always strive to appear *competent*.

Searching for an executive position must always include the preparation of a resume. General rules for resume writing include the fact that a resume should always be kept updated. Resumes should also represent the best that a person has to offer, displayed in the best possible manner.

When you have landed your position, it is important to bear in mind three sets of relationships that are going to condition the kind of existence that you'll have with that organization. These relationships include subordinates, peers, and superiors. A series of strategies has to be developed for use with each group. Organizational politics is going to be very competitive, but you can and should play the competitive game on your own terms. It is not necessary for you to violate your own moral standards in order to compete.

You should always maintain a running inventory on your skills, accomplishments, and deficiencies. This can be done by maintaining and keeping faithfully an inventory sheet each year.

THE THREE RULES FOR ACHIEVING AND MAINTAINING AN EXECUTIVE JOB

1. Your search for an executive position will involve two important methods: *strategy* and *tactics.* Strategy means finding out as much about the organization, its values, methods, and management as you can. Tactics means that you have studied all of the circumstances of a successful interview.
2. In your climb to the top, you will experience different kinds of relationships with three different groups: subordinates, peers, and superiors. For each group that you deal with, there are different strategies as well as different relationships.
3. Develop and maintain an inventory, year by year, of your goals, skills, accomplishments, and deficiencies.

EXERCISES FOR CHAPTER 9

1. Write someone else's resume. It could be a friend or relative or some famous person (get material from his or her biography). See how attractive you can make that person to a prospective employer.

2. Have interview sessions with friends. Set up some ground rules first. Especially important will be trying to answer questions that are unexpected.

3. Research a major corporation. Try to ascertain what its public image is like, what values it has, and what its management is like.

NOTES

1. Herbert E. Meyer, "Remodeling The Executive For The Corporate Climb," *Fortune,* July 16, 1979.

2. Another good resource is the recently published *Dress for Success* by T. J. Molloy.

3. Harold J. Leavitt, *Managerial Psychology.* University of Chicago Press, 3rd ed., 1972. p. 297.

4. David C. McClelland and David H. Burnham "Power is the Great Motivator" *Harvard Business Review on Human Relations,* Harper & Row, New York, 1979, p. 349.

Index

Abilities, for good executives, 67–88
  rules for developing, 86
  self-appraisal, 84–85
Advertising, roadside, 212–14
Affirmative action, 188
Agricultural Adjustment Act (*see* The Roosevelt Administration)
Albrecht, Karl, 160, 167n.
Alger, Horatio, 231
Amos (*see* "Famous Amos")
Anaximander, 131
Aristotle, 197
Arnold, Matthew, 123
Arthur D. Little, Inc., 205
Atlantic Community, The, 191
Authority, decision-making, 178–81
  entrenched, 111
Automation, 190
Automobile industry, regulated, 186
  See also individual companies

Bacon, Sir Francis, 123
Bailey, F. Lee, 48
Banking Reforms (*see* The Roosevelt Administration)
Barber, James D., 105, 115n.
Beecher, Henry Ward, 123
Behavior, managerial, 160
  organizational, 168
  See also Managers, functions
Bell and Howell Company, 216–18, 220
Bennett, Arnold, 124
Benson, Herbert, M.D., 222n.
Berle, Adolph, 215
Bonneville Dam, 97
"Brainstorming," 77, 197
Brushless shaving cream, 212
Bureaucracy, government, 171–72
Burma-Shave, company, 211–15, 220
  roadside jingles, 211–14
Burma-Vita Company (*see* Burma-Shave)
Burnham, David H., 240–241, 246n.

Butterfield, Alexander, 95

Cabinet-level agencies (U.S.), 169
Canada, 83, 101
Careers, government (*see*
    Government agencies)
Carnegie, Dale, 226
Carter, President Jimmy, 96, 172
Catastrophe Theory (*see* Thom,
    René)
Cervantes, 124
Chain stores, 100
Change, adventure or insecurity,
    91
  its constancy, 81, 136
Character, 105–108, 113
  characteristics of personality
    types described (Table 4–1),
    105
  presidential character, 105–108
Charles II, King of England, 83
Chesterfield, Lord, 124
Chopin, Frederic, 208
Chrysler Corporation, 182
Churchill, Sir Winston, 189, 204
Civil Service Commission, appeal
    and suit of A. E. Fitzgerald,
    95–96
Civil Service Reform Act, Senior
    Executive Service, 172–73
  "Whistleblower Protection," 96
Civil Service reforms, 62
Civilian Conservation Corps (*see*
    The Roosevelt
    Administration)
Climb from within, The, 233–44
  relationships on the way up,
    234–42
    with the boss, 238–42
    with peers, 236–38
    with subordinates, 234–36
Clustering (*see* Luck)
Cohen, Benjamin, 215
Columbia University, 214
Communication, 32–34, 35
  as power, 33, 35
Communist societies, managerial
    initiative, 149–50

trade relations with the West,
    191
  Yugoslavia's worker-
    management teams, 79
  See also Socialist societies
Compact car (*see* The Henry J.)
Computers (*see* Management
    revolution)
Conflict, creative, 90–91
Confluence (*see* Luck)
Congress (U.S.), C-5A aircraft
    hearings, 95–96
  and the First Amendment, 174
  and the Freedom of
    Information Act, 188
  relations with corporations, 156
  and the Roosevelt
    Administration. 214
Connor, General Fox, 159
Constitution (U.S.), Fifth and
    Fourteenth Amendments,
    173
  First Amendment, 174
Consumer Product Safety
    Commission, 188
Cooperation, among executives,
    181–185, 193
Corcoran, Thomas, 215
Corporate clone, The, 89, 112
"Corporate image," 89
Corporations, 89–91, 173–74
  and Anti-Trust Laws, 173
  and change, 89–91
  conglomerates, 174
  constitutional protections, 173
  multinationals, 174
  structures, 173–74
Cost overruns, 95
Creative Education Foundation,
    197
Creative individuals, 209–18
Creative organizations, 209–18
Creative problem solving, steps,
    199–207
  collection and use of facts,
    199–203
    "brainstorming," 202

morphological analysis,
200–201
sequential analysis, 201–203
checklists, 201–202
serendipity, 202–203
working models, 200–201
deliberation, 204–206
the Gordon technique, 205
gestation, 203–204
judgment, 206–207
Gestalt psychology, 206
testing, 207
solution, 207
Creativity, 196–221
developing creative
imagination, 197–98
rules for, 221
hindrances to, 207–209
Crisis, management of, 29–32, 35
situations, 30–32
environment, 31–32
functional, 32
leadership, 31
personnel, 30–31
Cybernetics, 190

Decision-making, 67–69, 92–93,
151–55, 165, 178–81, 190
computer assistance, 190
how managers make decisions
(Figure 6–1), 153
manager-subordinates
relationship, 178–181
continuum of
manager-nonmanager
behavior (Figure 7–1), 179
nonconformist thinking, 92–93
objectives-setting roles of
managers (Table 6–1), 152
steps analyzed, 151–155
See also Managers, functions
Decision-making authority,
delegation of, 27–28
Decisions, 67–69, 190
computer assistance, 190
incremental, 67–69
mixed, 67–69
rational, 67–69

Dedication, 145–48, 164, 165
enthusiasm, 145
goal-oriented activity, 145
Webster's definition, 145
Defense, Department of, 92
Depressed areas, entrepreneurs
in, 100–101
Developing countries, 191
Dingee, Alexander, 100–101, 113
"Dirty-tricks," 143
Discipline, self, 148–50, 164
and morale, 149
Dissent, 90–91
Doudney, Sarah, 123
Drake, Edwin L., 208
Drucker, Peter F., 135, 140n., 160,
167n., 176, 191, 194n.

ECCO (Enthusiasm, Courage,
Confidence, Optimism), 57
Economic crisis, 169
survival, 196
Economic and social reform
(U.S.) (*see* The Roosevelt
Administration)
Edison, Thomas A., 159
Education, Department of, 169
Eisenhower, President Dwight D.,
159, 167n.
Electronic Data Processing (*see*
Management revolution)
Elizabeth I, Queen of England,
123
Emerson, Ralph Waldo, 65, 87n.
Energy crisis, 169
Environment, of the organization,
110–11, 113
Environmental Protection
Agency, 156, 188
Estes, Pete, 181, 183
Europe, industrial and
technological progress, 196
European Common Market, 191
Excellence, 145–46
in leadership, 71
Executive behavior, 62–66, 81–86
awareness, 81–86
communication skills, 65

creativity, 81–86
delegation of authority, 63–64
enthusiasm, 65
failures, reasons for, 63–66
inflexibility, 63
innovation, 81–86
mobility, 62–63
temperament, 66
time-management, 64–65
Executive leadership, 11–12,
    14–16, 62
  benefits from, 14–16
  formula for achieving, 11–14
  qualities of, 12
  shortage of, 15
  talent needed, 62
Executive personality types,
    102–105, 113
  characteristics of personality
    types described (Table 4–1),
    105
  company man, 102
  craftsman, 102–103
  gamesman, 103–104
  jungle fighter, 103
  maverick, 104–105
Executive position, achieving and
    maintaining it, 224–46
  basic rules, 245
Executive's new role, The, 187–89
  defender of the organization,
    187
  pressures for social
    responsibility, 187–89
  public relations, 188
  See also Managers, functions
Executives, sabbatical leaves, 83

"Famous Amos" (chocolate chip
    cookies), 82
Farmer mail order market, The,
    100
Fayol, Henri, 75, 150
Fear, obstacle to advancement,
    122, 129–30
Federal Bureau of Investigation,
    170

Federal Emergency Relief Act
    (*see* The Roosevelt
    Administration)
Federal regulatory agencies, 172,
    188
Fiedler, Arthur, 123
Firestone, Harvey, 90
Firestone Tire and Rubber
    Company, 90
Fitzgerald, A. Ernest, 95–96, 113
Fixing schemes, 95
Ford, Henry, 20, 92
Ford, Henry II, 92
Ford Motor Company, 92, 182
Foreign competition, American
    steel industry, 173
Fortune magazine, 224
Frankfurter, Felix, 215
Frazer, Joe, 98
Free enterprise system, The, 148,
    173, 220
  and imagination, 220
  and responsibility, 148
  See also Modern industrial
    societies
Freedom of Information Act,
    The, 188
Future, sensitivity to, The, 81,
    136–37, 138

Gardner, John W., 145, 148, 166n.
General Motors, 75, 92, 156, 159,
    181–83
  Pontiac and Oldsmobile
    Divisions, 182
Goals, 95
  See also Objectives
Good management skills (*see*
    Management revolution)
Good timing (*see* Timing)
Gordon, W. J., 205
Government agencies, 169–73
  careers in, 170–73
  executive positions, 62
Government services, 169
Grand Coulee Dam, 97
Grant, General Ulysses S., 92–93

Great Depression, The, (*see* Wall Street)
Groups, and the individual, 91

Haldeman, H. R., 95
Harvard, Business School, 92
  College, 94
  graduates' occupation questionnaire, 54
  University, 189
Hawkeye Company, The, 97
Hawley, Cameron, 70, 88n.
Heller, Joseph, 204
Henry J - compact car, The, 98
Henry J. Kaiser Company, The, 97–98
Herzberg, Frederick, 79, 88n.
Hoover Dam, 97
Hudson's Bay Company, 83
Hughes, Howard, 20

"Ice King, The," (*see* Tudor, Frederick)
"Ideaphoria," 209
Image consultants, 224–25
  See also Self-image
Imagination, 195–223
  industrialized nations, 196
  United States, past success, 196
  present challenge, 196
  See also Creativity
Imagination quotient, guidelines for improvement, 218–29
Individualism, 90–91, 93, 101, 112–13
Information, importance for managers, 83–84
Integrity, 142–45, 164, 165
  acquiring it, steps, 144–45
  Webster's definition, 142
Internal Revenue Code, 174
Internal Revenue Service, 170
Interstate Commerce Commission, 169
Interview (*see* Job interview)
Inventory (*see* Self-inventory)
I.Q. (*see* Imagination quotient)

Jaeger, Werner, 140n.
Japan, industrial and technological progress, 81, 146, 196
Job interview, 228–32
  factors for success, 229–32
Johnson, Samuel, 123, 143
Johnson-O'Connor Foundation, 209
Jung, C. G., 42
Justice, Department of, Anti-Trust Division, 173

Kaiser, Edgar, 97
Kaiser, Henry J., 96–98, 113
Kaiser-Frazer Automobiles, 98
Kennedy, Joseph P., 51
Kennedy, President John F., 92
Kipling, Rudyard, 30, 37n.
"Knowledge workers" (*see* Specialists)

Lawyers' Weekly Report, 227
Leadership, 13–14, 27–28, 177–81
  centralized, 27
  consultative, 27–28
  creative, 27–28
  decentralized, 28
  executive (*see* Executive leadership)
  quality, 144
  styles, 177–81
  successful, 13–14
  team, 27–28
Leadership and management, principles, 11
Leavitt, Harold J., 239, 246n.
Lebhar, Godfrey M., 140n.
Legislatures, and public service agencies, 170–71
Leibnitz, 123
Levinson, Harry, 75, 88n., 143, 166n.
Little, Arthur D. (*see* Arthur D. Little, Inc.)
Lobbying, 171–72

Lombardi, Vince, 104
Loyalty, 240–41
Luck, 38–61
  confluence theory, 42–44, 58
  enhancing your own, 41–61
  and human will, 39–41, 58
  learning from the past, 54–56, 58
    diary, use of, 55
    example, 55
  Murphy's Law, 53
  network of connections, 49–51, 58
  positive thinking (dreaming, wishing), 56–57
  preserving gains, 51–52, 58
  risking, 44–49, 58
  rules for becoming lucky, 59
  understanding it, 41–61
  Webster's definition, 39
  worry (vigilance), 52–53, 58

MacArthur, General Douglas, 92–93
McClelland, David C., 240–41, 246n.
Maccoby, Michael, 102, 115n.
Machiavelli, Niccolo, 21–23, 26, 37n.
McKeon, Richard, 222n.
McMurry, Robert N., 104, 115n.
McNamara, Robert S., 92
Madison Avenue, 211, 214
Mail, direct selling, 217
Mail order house, 99
Management, middle level jobs, 80, 190
Management, modern (see Management Science)
Management revolution, 190
  computers, 190
  electronic data processing, 190
  semi-conductors, 190
Management Science
  early, 150
  MBO, 141–42, 151, 159–65
  modern, 27, 151, 160

organizational behavior, 168
  participatory management, 151
  philosophy of management, 160
  POSDCORB, 150, 167n.
  schools of management, 141
Management skills, 66–80
  communicating, 72–75
  decision-making, 67–69
  directing, 71–72
  mobilizing followers, 69–71
  motivating, 77–80
  planning, 76–77
Management of yourself, 142, 164
Managerial behavior, 160
Managers, functions, 150–59, 165
  decision-maker, 151–55, 165
    how managers make decisions (Figure 6–1), 153
    steps analyzed, 151–55
  guardian, 155–57, 165
    crisis management, 157
    liason, i56–57
    monitor, 156
    negotiator, 156
    planner, 155
    teacher, exemplifier and mentor, 157–59
  See also Objectives
Marine Corps, officer training, 158
Marketing methods, 92
MBO, Management by Objectives, 141–42, 151, 159–65
  art and science of, 160–61
  danger of misuse, 164
  and measurable goals, 161–62
  techniques of, 161–64
  See also Management Science
Medici, the family, 21–22
Meyer, Herbert E., 224, 246n.
Mintzberg, Henry, 132, 140n.
Mobility, top executives, 62–63
Modern industrial society, role of imagination, 196, 220
Moley, Raymond, 214–15, 223n.
Molloy, T. J., 246n.
Money back guarantee, 99

Montgomery, Field Marshall
Bernard L., 92–93
Montgomery Ward, 99–100
Movie camera (*see* Bell and
Howell)
Murphy's Law, 25, 53, 59

Nader, Ralph, 186
Naderism (see Public relations)
Napoleon, 11, 123
National Industrial Recovery Act
(*see* The Roosevelt
Administration)
Network (*see* Luck)
New Deal Legislation (*see* The
Roosevelt Administration)
New York Times, 187
Newsweek, 196
Nixon, President Richard M., 95
Nonconformity, 89–115
rules for, 114

Objectives, 151–59, 165
decision-making, 151–55
how managers make
decisions (Figure 6–1), 153
steps analyzed, 151–55
goals for good managers,
150–51
objectives-setting roles of
managers (Table 6–1), 152
roles analyzed, 151–59
rules for setting objectives, 165
Odell, Allan, 212–13
Odell, Leonard, 212–13
Ohmann, O. H., 146, 166n.
Oil cartels, 191
Oldsmobile Division (*see* General
Motors)
Opportunity, 124–31, 138
OPTing to Move, formula, 124
rules for, 125–38
Organization man, The, 89, 112
Organizational behavior, study
of, 168
Organizational ladder, The,
233–44
Organizational structure and
behavior, 177–89, 193

control, 177–81
centralized v. decentralized,
177
continuum of
manager-nonmanager
behavior (Figure 7–1), 179
delegation of
decision-making authority,
178–81
leadership style, 177–81
manager-subordinates
relationship, 178–81
intraorganizational behavior,
181–87
coalitions, 183–85
competition, 182
conflict and creativity, 181–82
group constituencies, 182–83
ideology (goals and values),
182–87
and the public image, 186
public relations, 186, 188
social responsibility, 187–89
affirmative action, 188
consumerism, 188
law suits, 188
Naderism, 188
regulatory agencies, 188
revolutionary developments,
187
Organizational theory, 75
See also Management Science
Organizations, 168–94
behavioral and structural
changes, 174, 176–77
future of, 189–92, 193
conglomerates, 191
Cybernetics, 190
international trade, 191
multinationals, 191
segmented horizontal
structure, 191
specialists needed, 191
technological innovation, 192
private, 169, 173–74
contrasted with public,
173–74

recent corporate
developments, 173–74
public, 169–73
Osborn, Alex, 197, 222n.
O'Shaughnessy, Arthur, 57, 61n.

Parliament of Europe, 191
Pascal, Blaise, 42
Patton, General George S., 69
Percy, William Alexander, 61n.
Personality traits, 24–26, 105
characteristics of personality
traits described (Table 4–1),
105
"Pet Rocks," 82
Peterson, Peter G., 216–17
Philip Morris Company, 214
Philosophy of management (*see*
Management Science)
Planning, major goals, 76–77
alternatives, 77
contingencies, 77
See also Managers, functions
Polaroid cameras, 195–96
Politics, intraorganizational,
182–84, 193, 237
Pontiac Division (*see* General
Motors)
POSDCORB (*see* Management
Science)
Potential, fulfilling it, 141
Power, 17–36
centralized v. decentralized,
20–21
chain of command, 18
controlled aggression, 33–34, 35
and decision-making, 20
four keys to, 35–36
Machiavellian, 21–24, 26
positive and negative aspects,
17
and responsibility, 20–21, 35
rules for use of, 17–21
Presidents (U.S.), 107
See also individual names
Problem solving, nonconformist
approaches, 93–102

See also Creative problem
solving
Protestant ethic, The, 102
Public agencies (*see* Government
agencies)
Public image, the organization's,
186
Public relations, 187–88
the media, 187
Naderism and consumerism,
188
politicians, 187
pressure groups, 187
specialists, 188
Public service organizations,
174–76, 193
and the First Amendment,
174
the growth sector of society,
176
need for good managers, 176
services of, 175
social responsibility, 187–89,
193
tax exempt, 174
Public utilities, monopoly, 173

Regulation, automobile industry,
186
See also Federal regulatory
agencies
Research and development, 196
Responsibility revolution, The
(*see* Social responsibility)
Resume (job application), 232–33
basic rules, 233
Rivalry, friendly, 143
Roadside signs (*see* Advertising)
Rommel, Field Marshal Erwin,
92–93
Roosevelt, President Franklin D.,
204, 214, 215, 216, 220
Roosevelt Administration, The,
214–16, 220
New Deal legislation, 215
Rosenwald, Julius, 99
Rowsome, Frank, Jr., 222n.

Safety and Health
Administration, Office of,
188
Santayana, George, 54, 61n.
Schools of Management (*see*
Management Science)
Sears, Roebuck, and Company,
99–100
Self-image, improvement
strategy, 225–28
appearance, 225–26
being informed, 225
communicating, 226–27
community service, 228
image consultants, 224–25
publications, 227
Self-inventory, accomplishments
and deficiencies, 242–44,
245
example, 243
Semi-conductors (*see*
Management revolution)
Seriality (*see* Synchronicity)
Service, 147–48, 164
standard of sacrifice, 147–48
teamwork, 148
Shakespeare, William, 40, 61n.,
109–110, 115n., 117
Sharpe, R. L., 123
"Show and Tell" (*see* Job
interview)
Sloan, Alfred P., 75, 159
Social responsibility, corporate,
187–89
public service institutions, 189
Socialist societies, 196, 220
South Africa, 189
Specialists ("Knowledge
workers"), 191–92
Specialization, 27
Steel industry (American), 173
Steiner, Gary, 209–210, 222n.,
223n.
Stewart, Jimmy, 90
Stockholders, the company's
dealers, 217–18
Strategy geniuses, 92

Style, 93–113
"M.O." (*modus operandi*) of
managers, 102
"Sunset Laws," 170
Supreme Court (U.S.), 173, 188,
215
Sweden (*see* Volvo)
Synchronicity, 42

Tables and Figures, 105, 152, 153,
179
*Characteristics of Personality
Types Described* (Table
4–1), 105
*Continuum of
Manager-Nonmanager
Behavior* (Figure 7–1),
179
How Managers Make Decisions
(Figure 6–1), 153
*Objectives-Setting Roles of
Managers* (Table 6–1), 152
Teamwork, 26–29, 35
Technological revolution, 190–92
and human skills, 192
Television, corporate sponsorship
of public service programs,
217
Temperament, for leadership,
112
Tennessee Valley Authority (*see*
The Roosevelt
Administration)
Thales, 131
Thom, René, catastrophe theory,
43
Time, executive allocation of,
132–33
future time, planning for,
121–22
opportunity, 124–31
passage of, quotations
concerning, 123–24
past time, analyzed, 117–18
present time, attitudes toward,
119–21
the value of, 122–24
Time-management, 132–36

improvement guidelines,
133–36
planning schedules, 136
Timing, 116–40
formula for, 124–25
OPTion to Move, 125
rules for achieving a sense of,
125–29
Toynbee, Mrs. Paget, 222n.
Trade, international, 191
Tradition, 111
Trucking industry, regulation of,
169
Tudor, Frederick, 94–95, 113
Tugwell, Rexford, 215

Urban middle class market, 100

Values, 108–110, 113
clarification questionnaire, 109
Venture Founders, Inc., 100–101
Volvo, team assembly, 78–79

Von Fange, Eugene K., 222n.
Wall Street, crash of October,
1929, 51
See also The Roosevelt
Administration
Walpole, Horace, 202
Washington, General George,
92–93
Webster's Dictionary, 39, 142, 145
Wells, H. G., 116–17, 140n.
Western societies, 196–97
Western technology, 191
"Whistleblower protection," 96
Wiener, Norbert, 190
Wilson, Woodrow, 124
Wood, Robert E., 99–100
Work ethic, The, 104

Young, Edward, 123
Yugoslavia (see Communist
societies)

Zaleznik, Abraham, 184, 194n.